The

Chinese

Garden

GARDEN TYPES FOR CONTEMPORARY
LANDSCAPE ARCHITECTURE

Bianca Maria Rinaldi

The

Chinese

Garden

With a Foreword by Franco Panzini

Birkhäuser
Basel

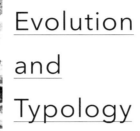

The
Chinese
Garden

Evolution and Typology

Composition and Effects

Elements

Reconfiguring the Chinese Garden

Short Portraits of Parks and Gardens

APPENDIX

Foreword

After a long period of near-oblivion, the Chinese Garden seems to be entering a fruitful new season. Recent years have brought many books and articles on the subject, and international periodicals now regularly publish landscape projects conceived in China.

The development leading to this recent success of the Chinese Garden outside China has been decidedly irregular, almost as though it were following the principles – so influential in Chinese Gardens – of *fengshui,* where linearity has no place.

In the 17th and 18th centuries, when a few European visitors – Catholic missionaries, first of all – gained access to the court of Beijing, capital of a willfully isolated country, they discovered gardens whose composition was based on evocation of natural landscape features reproduced in iconic and allusive forms. Their letters describing those highly original gardens, published in the West, contributed not only to the birth of the Landscape Garden in England, but aroused a gardening sinophilia; images of Chinese Gardens appeared on porcelain and tapestries, and fantastic imitations were created in aristocratic parks à la mode. But with the political decline of the empire toward the end of the 18th century, international consideration of China changed, and the country was no longer seen as a place of ancient culture but rather as an appetizing prey. During the long eclipse that began with the dissolution of the empire, the gardening tradition was all but forgotten.

It was only thanks to the general improvement in communications and above all the development of photography that documentation of that tradition became available to the world. In 1909, the genial French banker, philanthropist, traveler and dreamer Albert Kahn launched the project of collecting a photographic record of the entire earth. The resulting collection provided glimpses of ancient gardens, including a series of photographs made in China by the French photographer Stéphane Passet in 1912. These melancholy images, made with pioneering color technique the same year the last emperor abdicated and the Republic was proclaimed, reveal an ancient world about to disappear. Thanks to them, we can see the majestic imperial gardens of Beijing.

Decades later, the first panorama of Chinese Gardens was given to the world by a northerner, Osvald Sirén, a great early scholar of Chinese art history. When he became a professor of fine arts at Stockholm University in 1908 he also, like many European intellectuals of that period, became a student of theosophy; it was perhaps for that reason that he developed an interest in Asia and particularly in Chinese art. The expertise he developed led to his nomination in 1926 as curator of Chinese painting and sculpture at the National Museum of Art in Stockholm.

Sirén was a passionate photographer. During his four visits to China and Japan between 1918 and 1935, he was able to document the gardens of Beijing, Hangzhou and Suzhou. His records of those fragile green spaces have great value and were the basis of his *Gardens of China,* a book published in 1949 but written in Lidingö during the war; in this island town north of Stockholm Sirén had a country retreat featuring its own little Chinese garden. *Gardens of China* is not only an extraordinary collection of photographs, but also a scholarly text on the ways Chinese Gardens were composed, ways Sirén began to study both in terms of modalities and of general organization.

Sirén understood both the decorative and the symbolic value of the gardens' huge rocks, as well as the complementary value of the water, and he also understood that the mode of composition of a Chinese Garden was inspired by the way painted landscape scrolls were unrolled for viewing: "The Chinese garden can never be completely surveyed from a certain point. It consists of more or less isolated sections which must be discovered gradually and enjoyed as the beholder continues his stroll… he is led on into a composition that is never completely revealed." He noted compositional tricks, like the idea of "borrowing scenery", which was a technique of framing sections of the landscape outside the garden so as to bring it inside, with the ultimate aim of making the garden appear larger than it actually was.

Sirén's pioneering work was followed by many other books which dealt at least partially with the techniques used to create Chinese Gardens, beginning with the first modern treatment by a Chinese author, the scholar Liu Dunzhen, *Classical Gardens of Suzhou*, published in a Chinese edition in 1979, then in a partial English translation in 1982 and eventually as a complete English edition in 1993.

With the spread of oriental philosophies and literature, which undoubtedly do influence these gardens, spatial organization has come to be viewed as secondary to the metaphysical component. Rarely has there been an analysis of the material elements constituting a Chinese Garden, aimed at discovering the rules of distribution, proportions and relations guiding the use of those elements. Philosophical, religious or literary interest has prevailed, creating confusion between the references behind a composition and the compositional techniques used to elicit the desired effects. To paraphrase a maxim borrowed from another context, the message got confused with the medium.

It is precisely in the ways and strategies of composition that the Chinese Garden features characteristics that are unique in the history of gardens. These become fully evident in an analysis of the physical apparatus created within the garden's space in order to inform the visitors' visual and mental perceptions. Investigation of the material ways in which Chinese Gardens were engineered can offer ideas for current research and design – elaborating on the Chinese Garden's capacity for constructing a narrative, for integrating with the built environment, but also for its manner of embosoming the individual in a natural system. These gardens foreshadow environmental sustainability. Evocation of the elements and landscapes of the Chinese Garden is not merely a delicate historical note, but parallels today's interest in environmental requalification and reconstruction of damaged habitats. Far from being a precious intellectual exercise, the search for a harmonious microcosm constitutes a vigorous enunciation of the need for sustainability in all creations. Studying the compositional methods of Chinese Gardens is not only a deeper way to understand one of the great adventures in humanity's relation with nature, but also an important contribution to the evolution of contemporary landscape architecture.

Franco Panzini

Chapter 1

Evolution

and

Typology

In the second act of *Turandot*, Giacomo Puccini's unfinished opera written in the early 1920s and set in fabled Imperial-era China, three ministers of state improbably named Ping, Pong and Pang are complaining about the rigid life they are forced to lead at the court of the beautiful and cruel princess Turandot. They would prefer to live in their peaceful country homes far from the capital:

"I have a house in Honan
with a little pond so blue,
all surrounded by bamboo.
And here I am, wasting my life,
racking my brains over sacred books..."

Puccini composed *Turandot* at a time when Europe had long been fascinated by the exotic Orient, and the libretto's description of the private garden of one of those officials shows clearly what Westerners saw as the essence of the green architectures of the Far East: naturalness (I-1). The libretto mentions bamboo and a little pond, stereotypical features of a Chinese Garden, but in previous centuries many Western visitors to China – merchants, travelers, missionaries, ambassadors – had far more thoroughly described the parks they had been able to see. These visitors always commented on the natural aspect of these gardens, as well as on what appeared to be a complete lack of order in their plans, something far different from the Western approach (I-2).

I-1   I-2

I-3   I-4

Artificiality and Naturalness

Western visitors, in their accounts and descriptions, were often attempting to outline the inherent characteristics of Chinese Gardens, as distinct from all other gardens. Their "natural appearance", implying "irregularity" of forms and thus an apparent general confusion, was a constant theme. But the French Jesuit missionary Pierre-Martial Cibot (1727-1780) explained how, in fact, this irregularity was entirely calculated, an artifice intended to evoke the simplicity of a natural landscape[1] (I-3; I-4). The apparent simple appearance of the Chinese Garden, with its anti-urban quality, its placid hamlets of pavilions, its silences, suggested to the Jesuit the image of a rural naturalness. Summing up the Chinese Garden's main, common characteristics, he wrote that "the Gardens of China are a studied but natural imitation of the various beauties of the countryside, in hills, valleys, gorges, pools, little plains, sheets of water, brooks, isles, rocks, grottoes, old caves, plants and flowers"[2]. The multiple ways in which nature's scene was evoked had the purpose of calling up emotional reactions, as Cibot explained: "A garden thus should be the living and animated image of all that one finds there [in nature], to engender in the soul the same sentiments, and to satisfy the eyes with the same pleasure"[3].

The ability of the Chinese to grasp the many forms through which "real" nature could present itself in the artificial context of the garden was, for Westerners, quite striking. The Englishman Lord George Macartney (1737-1806), who in 1793 led the first British embassy to the Qianlong Emperor, commenting on the design of the imperial garden of *Yuanming yuan*, "Garden of Perfect Brightness", near Beijing (I-5), noted in his journal: "[The Chinese gardener's] point is to change everything from what he found it... and introduce novelty in every corner... If there be a smooth flat, he varies it with all possible conversions. He undulates the surface, raises it in hills, scoops it into valleys and roughens it with rocks. He softens asperities, brings amenity into the wilderness, or animates the tameness of an expanse by accompanying it with the majesty of a forest"[4].

I-1: Olympic Forest Park, Beijing. The concept of the park deals with an investigation into the sense of naturalness which first engendered Chinese Gardens.

I-2: Yu yuan, "Garden to Please", Shanghai. A pavilion overlooking one of the many ponds of the garden.

I-3: Canglang ting, "Surging Waves Pavilion", Suzhou. The pond is bordered with rocks.

I-4: Yu yuan. Rocks simulating a crest of a hill are arranged around the reflecting pool.

I-5: Tang Dai and Shen Yuan, *Forty Views of Yuanming yuan*, 1747, vol. 1, view n. 4, *Luyue kaiyun*, "Engraving the moon and carving the clouds". Ink and watercolor on silk.

I-5

If we wanted to condense into a slogan Chinese garden design's distinctive attribute through time, thus identifying a unique compositional formula, it could be this: artificiality in nature[5] (I-6). Chinese Gardens show an apparent natural simplicity, an endeavor to restore, sometimes in rather tiny areas, the rhythms and diversity of nature. Occasionally this result is achieved through a concentration on a few elements, but more often nature's multi-faceted appearance is evoked through diversification of the garden's aspects.

The presence of different and often surprising settings, which follow one another without any apparent hierarchy, makes the spatial perception of the garden difficult. But, despite their apparent confusion, Chinese Gardens are in fact organized and ordered. They are places where the visitors' senses are continually stimulated through compositional effects intended to awaken curiosity, surprise and aesthetic appreciation. Chinese Gardens are slow. Like films, their effects are built through a sequence of different scenes and settings; separated by screens, walls and doorways, theirs is an unfoldment, a revelation by degrees. Chinese Gardens are never perceived in their entirety. Like music and poetry, they are built through progression, variation and repetition of theme, rhythm and elements, which make them coherent and harmonious. These can be considered the common characteristics defining the Chinese Garden type through time.

In this composite character derived from the natural landscape, Chinese Gardens show analogies with traditions developed in other historical and geographical contexts.

Chinese Gardens are in fundamental harmony with Japanese Gardens, whose origin was influenced by the Chinese tradition (I-7). The two types share the intent of representing the basic characters of the natural environment in miniaturized and metaphorical form. Where they differ is in the manner of that representation. Japanese Gardens express a predilection for a formal sobriety of rural inspiration, a compositional understatement which reached its peak in Zen monasteries toward the end of the 15th century with the creation of *karesansui*, dry gardens made up of a few essential elements: rocks, gravel, moss. The great aristocratic Japanese Gardens, organized as itineraries through different scenes as in China, are more fluid in moving from one scene to another; they do not adopt those explicitly artificial visual devices of Chinese tradition like walls of separation between zones of the garden (I-8).

I-6: House of Consequa in the suburbs of Canton.

I-7: Koishikawa Korakuen, Tokyo. Built starting from 1629, the garden was inspired by the collection of different scenes typical of Chinese Gardens.

I-8: Shugakuin Rikyu, Kyoto. Built in the mid-17th century, the garden of this great imperial villa is an example of a Stroll Garden, designed as fluid itineraries through different scenes.

I-9: Stowe, Buckinghamshire. Both Chinese and English Landscape Garden traditions share an appreciation for a constructed naturalness.

Evolution and Typology

The similarity of Chinese Gardens with the English Landscape Garden at a first glance is surprising. Yet the celebration of naturalness shared by both traditions was engendered by quite different motives. The English Landscape Garden was born of an almost epic exaltation of the productive countryside; it is a romantic presentation of nature lived in and transformed by men and women through the course of time. The Chinese Garden, by contrast, represents the superior natural order which human beings belong to and to which it is right for them to submit: at least for the time when they are in the garden (I-9).

Historical Chinese Gardens are linked with their contemporary version and current trends in composition by the way these both feature water as an important presence, and both emphasize naturalness. This connection is not limited to formal similarities, and even moves beyond differences in metaphysical interpretation, because both the traditional and the contemporary approach are based on the recognition of the innate human need to maintain contact with nature's vitality, even if experienced in a distilled form, as happens in a garden.

Ethics

The philosophical and metaphysical historical context which created the palimpsest of meanings implicit in the Chinese Garden is characterized by two main doctrines: Confucianism and Daoism[6]. These two philosophical systems were born in the same period, the 6th century BC, a period of great political and social changes. Their origins lay in the teachings of Kongfuzi, "Master Kong", whom the West knows as Confucius (551-479 BC), and Laozi (6th century BC), the "Old Master", a legendary figure, considered as the author of the main Daoist foundational texts.

Confucianism as a group of philosophical doctrines engendered a political ethic rather than a religion. Social relations and obligations were central to its teachings, and the underlying principle was that only in society could an individual reach self-fulfillment; life's ultimate purpose was considered in function of the role and activity of the individual. The family, as the original, spontaneous and natural form of association, was taken as a model for society.

Confucianism looked at man working in a definite context, in society and within the family. Daoism, based on the principle of the unity of the cosmos, taught rather that man belonged to a vaster order of things: the purpose of life was to seek harmony with the forces of nature. Both conceptions influenced gardens in China. The garden, as part of the family dwelling, was a place for social relations, but as a protected and isolated place it was also a space for

the meditation and contemplation of nature. This double philosophical inspiration was even more apparent in the radical juxtaposition of the conceptions of domestic architecture and of the garden: the former followed a geometric matrix based on symmetry and hierarchical relations among the parts, while the latter remained rather the realm of spontaneity and imagination (I-10). In proposing a connection with the natural world, the garden maintained a complete formal autonomy, which neither had its source in the architecture of the main building nor was subordinate to it, as instead was the case in the Western tradition (I-11). If the domestic structure responded to Confucian principles, the green open space, in its search for a concentrated and allusive natural quality, was rather a response to the dictates of Daoism and Buddhism, the latter being a later cultural and religious import from India, spreading into China from the 1st century AD onwards.

This apparent separation of references did not produce any dichotomy. China had an assimilative attitude to religion: Confucian geometry was joined, through Daoism and Buddhism, to a mystical appreciation of nature as expressed in garden design (I-12). In the heart of Chinese cities, private gardens attached to urban dwellings integrated a *summa* of Confucian, Daoist and Buddhist ethics: they were created by high officials with the purpose of finding moments of calm and contemplative appreciation of nature without distancing themselves from their duties toward their families and the state.

1 Entrance Hall	9 Ancient Five Pines Courtyard	16 Twin Fragrance Celestial House
2 Ancestral Hall	10 Pavilion of True Delight	17 Fan-shaped Pavilion
3 Hall of Joyous Feasts	11 Hall of Faint Fragrance and Thin Shadows	18 Pavilion in Memory of Wen Tianxiang
4 Small Square Hall	12 Stone Boat	19 Imperial Stele Pavilion
5 Hall Bowing to the Mountains Peaks and Facing the Cyprus Trees	13 Flying Waterfall Pavilion	20 Tower of Tall Slender Bamboo
6 Chamber Lying in the Clouds	14 Pavilion in the Heart of the Lake	21 Hall of Standing in the Snow
7 Tower with View of Mountains	15 Asking the Plum Trees Tower	
8 Lotus Flower Hall		

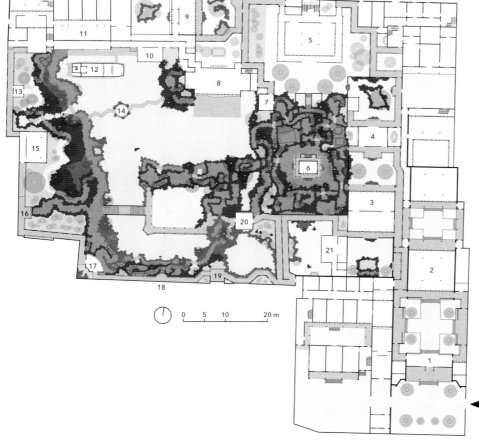

I-10: Wangshi yuan, "Garden of the Master of the Fishing Nets", Suzhou. A complex of pavilions in the inner part of the garden.

I-11: Shizi lin, "Lion Grove", Suzhou. Plan of the garden.

I-12: Yu yuan, "Garden to Please", Shanghai. Several pavilions are scattered through the many rock arrangements of the garden.

I-13: Xihu, "West Lake", Hangzhou. One of the three artificial islets of the lake.

Origins and Spatial Evolution

The Gardens of the Ancient Dynasties

The most remote precedents of Chinese Gardens were the royal hunting enclosures and animal preserves of the earliest dynasties[7]. The first reports of hunting preserves come from the Xia, Shang (c. 1600-1050 BC) and Zhou (c. 1050-256 BC) kingdoms, partly mythical dynasties having fenced properties featuring watercourses and pools, as well as wild animals and pavilions for court ceremonies. The habit of possession of animal preserves continued in time to be considered an attribute of royalty.

The empire was constituted in 221 BC, when the ruler of the state of Qin, having unified the country, declared himself the sovereign of China with the name Shihuangdi, "First Emperor" (reigned 221-206 BC); he established his capital at Xianyang, northwest of the modern city of Xi'an. It was near Xianyang that the first great park was created: *Shanglin*, "Supreme Forest". In addition to using it as a hunting preserve, the emperor had reconstructed fragments of gardens and palaces of the lands he had conquered, and to underscore the symbolic value of the park, he also gathered there animals and plants offered as tribute from vassal states.

The following dynasty, the Han (206 BC-220 AD), built its capital near the site of the capital of the Qin. The new center was called Chang'an (today's Xi'an); it was a lively cosmopolitan city, commercially influential as the place where what became known as the Silk Road began. The *Shanglin* park, inherited from the preceding emperor, was expanded and enriched by the sixth emperor of the Han dynasty, who ascended to the throne with the name Wudi (reigned 141-87 BC). There he brought plants and animals from distant lands, and had pavilions and little temples built, as well as a great artificial body of water, named Kunming Lake. Even though it remained mainly a hunting park, *Shanglin* became a miniature of the empire itself, with wooded heights, watercourses and pools. That was how one of the characteristics of China's garden culture came to be developed through time: the aesthetic of a collection of landscapes.

In that park, Wudi had an original composition built, destined to be replicated many times in later periods: the Islands of the Immortals. According to legend, the Immortals were semi-divine beings who, thanks to the practice of magic, had managed to acquire eternal life; they were thought to live in richly wooded mountainous islands beyond the coasts of China. The emperor decided to have those places represented in his park, creating three little islands in an artificial pool called Taiye Lake (I-13).

During the Han the formation of a new elite of state functionaries – aristocratic scholars appointed to run the civil service after tough examinations based on Confucian classics – and the possibility of private ownership of land, which enabled wealthy families to expand their properties through acquisitions, set the stage for the spread of private gardens. The end of the Han dynasty led to the dissolution of the empire and general political instability under the Six Dynasties (220-589).

In contrast with the political turbulence of the times, or perhaps as a direct reaction to it, paintings of nature, architecture and the art of the garden were pervaded by an aesthetic of detached elegance and simplicity. Created in cities by aristocrats and high officials, private gardens were intended to express the Daoist tendency to evade the complexity of daily life, in a search for harmony with nature and unity with the universe. Instead of vast spaces where emperors exhibited wealth and political power, these gardens were intimate and protected places where it was possible to take temporary refuge from harsh social and political surroundings.

The search for ways to create an idyllic atmosphere for increasingly cultivated patrons led to an accentuation of the gardens' literary and evocative nature (I-14). Trees, groups of plants, little hills and islands were poetically composed to recall real landscapes. The evocation in gardens of famous Chinese landscapes became a habitual practice, promoting the invention of techniques for realizing artificial heights and bodies of water (I-15).

I-14: Shizi lin, "Lion Grove", Suzhou.
A micro-landscape of fragments of rocks and little plants, composed on a flat stone tray, is redolent of a natural landscape.

I-15: Huqiu shan, "Tiger Hill", Suzhou.
Miniature trees and rockeries are carefully arranged to evoke real cliff faces.

I-16: Suzhou. The city is crossed by a large number of canals.

I-17: Suzhou. The canal flowing along the southern perimeter of the Ou yuan, "Couple's Garden Retreat".

The Gardens of the Sui and the Tang

At the end of the 6th century, the Sui dynasty (581-618) reunited the country. The second emperor of this brief dynasty, Yangdi (ruled 604-617), made the city of Luoyang the eastern capital of the empire and had a huge park created nearby, *Xi yuan*, "West Garden". In it a brook wound its way through 16 small gardens before dashing into a great lake marked by three islands graced with pavilions. Other channels of water connected this central lake with smaller pools, and it was only through this dense navigable network that it was possible to reach the main palace, so that water was the protagonist of the garden.

The form of this river-style garden, created by a complex system of serpentine channels connecting its various parts, reflected the significant advances Imperial China had made in hydraulic engineering. The highest expression of this technological process was an impressive territorial achievement of the Sui dynasty: the Grand Canal.

This was not a single channel, but rather a complex system of waterworks connecting rivers, lakes and already existing canals, making a waterway which then was roughly 2,500 km long. From the city of Hangzhou, located south of the Yangtse River delta and famous for its production of silk, tea and salt and surrounded by China's best land for rice production, the channel went north toward the city of Suzhou; it turned toward the interior then to reach the Yellow River and the capitals Luoyang and Chang'an, thence proceeding northeast toward the area of today's Beijing. Dug between 605 and 611, the Grand Canal testified to the reunification of the Chinese Empire, of which it became the main communication artery [8] (I-16; I-17).

The following era, the Tang dynasty (618-907), was a period of great development and well-being for China, in particular of creativity in the arts and technology: it was at this time that gunpowder was invented. The parks of the Tang emperors imitated some features of the gardens of preceding dynasties, thus legitimizing their rule. Like the parks of the Qin and Han periods, the Tang imperial gardens were huge and contained vast collections of

plants, both native and exotic, fruit of the institutional practice of sending tributes to the imperial court from the provinces of the kingdom, their transport now being facilitated by the Grand Canal (I-18; I-19; I-20).

The central element of garden design continued to be water, as it had been under the Sui dynasty. The grand imperial park *Huaqing* created by the Xuanzong Emperor (reigned 712-756), sixth sovereign of the Tang dynasty, near the imperial city of Chang'an, at the foot of the Lishan hills, was an example. Sources of thermal water in the hills were enclosed within the park's perimeter, whose design was organized around a series of artificial basins. The late Tang period was marked by a widespread aesthetic interest for rocks taken out of lakes or rivers, or quarried in mountains. Single weather-beaten or particularly shapely rocks, curious in outline or color, were placed on sculpted pedestals, or placed inside pots and situated in the gardens (I-21; I-22). A great number of beautifully formed rocks could be admired in the *Pingquan zhuang*, "Pingquan Villa", a suburban garden built south of the city of Luoyang. Created in 825 by Li Deyu (787-850), one of the Tang dynasty's most important political figures, this garden was a sort of open-air cabinet of curiosities; exotic plants and trees and rocks of unusual and fantastic appearance from various zones of China formed the collection, whose owner had elaborated a proper catalogue for them[9].

I-18: Nan Lian Garden, Hong Kong. Opened in 2006, the public park is inspired by the garden style developed during the Tang dynasty.

I-19: Nan Lian Garden. Clusters of rocks of bizarre shape are composed among the vegetation to create a scenic view.

I-20: Nan Lian Garden. Water is the main element of the garden design; the park is organized around two artificial lakes connected by a winding stream and bordered with rocks.

I-21: Qianlong Garden within the Ningshou gong, "Palace of Tranquil Longevity", Forbidden City, Beijing. An enormous single rock placed on a sculpted marble pedestal is the visual highlight of this small courtyard.

I-22: Yu yuan, "Garden to Please", Shanghai. A stone composition overlooking an artificial pond; the central rock, called "Exquisite Jade Rock", emerges as the chief feature.

I-18

I-19   I-20

The Gardens of the Song and the Yuan

In the following centuries, under the Northern Song dynasty (960-1127)[10], this interest in rocks exploded, and the single rocks earlier praised by connoisseurs were now joined by entire rock compositions, which became a specific design element in Chinese Gardens (I-23). It was the imperial park *Genyue*, "Northeast Mountain Peak", which marked the beginning of a new garden style, where stone landscapes dominated. Commissioned by Huizong (reigned 1101-1125), eighth emperor of the Northern Song, *Genyue* was a vast park created in 1117 and 1118 in the city that had become the capital of the empire, Bianliang (today's Kaifeng), situated in the eastern part of China, in a plain south of the Yellow River. The park presented as its central scene the evocation of a famous natural landscape, that of the Phoenix Mountain, a height near the city of Hangzhou, in southeastern China.

The creation of the park served as an occasion for exploration of the diverse aesthetic possibilities of rocks, which in their various compositions presented the entire repertory of scenes from an ideal mountain landscape. Rock masses of elaborate shapes were brought together to form hillocks and valleys, steep slopes and little grottos, while a high double-peaked artificial mountain dominated the picture. A waterfall surged out of its side, leaping into a basin placed at the foot of the rocky composition (I-24).

The Huizong Emperor was an energetic collector of rocks, trees and exotic plants, which he exhibited in his imperial park. His collector's passion had led him to set up a special imperial office in the city of Suzhou, named "Flower and Rock Network". This was an efficient service in searching out and transporting rare geological and botanical specimens, transported by ship on the Grand Canal to the capital Bianliang, to enrich *Genyue*'s collections[11]. During the reign of the Song, the class of scholars emerged as the defining elite of intellectual enlightenment. Literati and high officials were the great creators of gardens in this period, to the degree that the Chinese Garden got its imprint as a scholarly icon.

Poems and writings about gardens composed by scholars and officials flourished under the Song dynasty, bearing witness to the importance gardens were assuming within Chinese society.

I-23: Liu yuan, "Lingering Garden", Suzhou. A great single rock from the Lake Tai, the "Cloud-capped Peak" stands 6.5 m high in an open courtyard, overlooking a little pond.

I-24: Yu yuan, "Garden to Please", Shanghai. A complex scene evoking a mountainous chain towering a lake.

I-25: Canglang ting, "Surging Waves Pavilion", Suzhou. A planted artificial hill hides a little pond, bordered by rocks and by a covered walkway.

I-26: Canglang ting. The garden features a unique characteristic: one of the pathways runs along an external canal bordering the garden.

I-23

I-24

One example is the *Luoyang mingyuan ji, Record of the Famous Gardens of Luoyang*, written about 1095 by Li Gefei (c. 1041-1106), in which the author, a distinguished classical scholar, described gardens in the city of Luoyang he had personally visited.

These were gardens to be discovered slowly; in the Dong Family's West Garden, for example, "a little path runs to the lake, south of which there is a hall facing a pavilion set high up. Though the hall is not grand it twists and winds far back so that visitors often lose themselves there"[12]. In other gardens, it was a surprising vista or an unexpected effect which prevailed. In the Dong Family's East Garden, marked by the presence of a large lake, "water spouts into the lake from all sides, but leaves by concealed exits; so it seems as though there are incessant cascades and yet the lake never overflows"[13]. In other gardens, the presence of elevated heights made it possible to embrace the landscape beyond; this was the case of the Hu Family Gardens north of the river, where "there is a terrace with views in every direction of more than thirty-five miles within which the Yi River winds and the Luo River meanders; dense forests are obscured by mist and clouds; high towers and winding verandas are one moment hidden, the next apparent; such as a painter after the utmost contemplation could not depict"[14].

In his descriptions, Li Gefei includes the vegetation used in the private gardens of the city, and mentions of junipers, pines, bamboos and cypresses recur, evergreen plants, therefore, while the rare but intense spots of color were due to flowering bushes and small trees – paulownias, peaches and plums – and to peonies which, Li Gefei writes, were planted in all of Luoyang's gardens: "Many flowers are cultivated in Luoyang but only one is just named as 'the flower', it is the tree-peony. In every garden peonies are grown"[15].

Many private gardens flourished in the prosperous southern regions, as in the city of Suzhou, one of the most populous of the empire. A successful trading place with a lively cultural life, Suzhou was one of the main stops along the Grand Canal, and the city itself was crossed by a network of navigable canals. Here was the *Canglang ting*, "Surging Waves Pavilion", a garden created in 1045 by the scholar Su Shunqin (1008-1048), after he had retired as an official (I-27). In its original composition, *Canglang ting* presented a very simple design, which played on the contrast between two artificial hills and a reflecting pond (I-25). Its main characteristic, however, was that it had been created alongside one of the canals crossing the city. A pavilion facing the canal made explicit this union between the space of the garden and that of the course of water outside[16] (I-26).

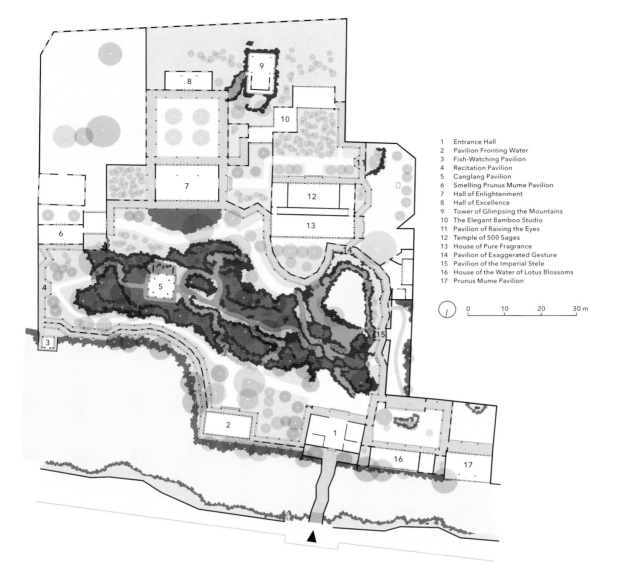

1 Entrance Hall
2 Pavilion Fronting Water
3 Fish-Watching Pavilion
4 Recitation Pavilion
5 Canglang Pavilion
6 Smelling Prunus Mume Pavilion
7 Hall of Enlightenment
8 Hall of Excellence
9 Tower of Glimpsing the Mountains
10 The Elegant Bamboo Studio
11 Pavilion of Raising the Eyes
12 Temple of 500 Sages
13 House of Pure Fragrance
14 Pavilion of Exaggerated Gesture
15 Pavilion of the Imperial Stele
16 House of the Water of Lotus Blossoms
17 Prunus Mume Pavilion

0   10   20   30 m

I-27: Canglang ting, "Surging Waves Pavilion", Suzhou. Plan of the garden.

I-28: Map of Dadu, modern Beijing, during the Yuan dynasty, with the Taiye Lake, the artificial lake excavated in the western part of the imperial city.

I-29: Beihai Park, Beijing. The artificial lake covering more than half of the entire park is dominated by the artificial hilly island called Qionghua dao, "Jade Islet".

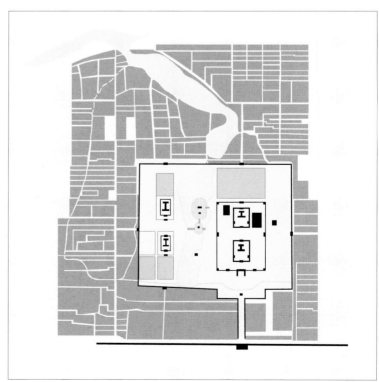

The Mongols, who conquered China in 1279, were no great garden-builders, but Khubilai Khan (reigned 1260-1294), who founded the Yuan dynasty (1279-1368), built Dadu, "The Great Capital", on the site of what is now Beijing[17]. There he began creating what later became part of the so-called *Beihai* and *Jingshan* Parks, by developing further the Taiye Lake, an artificial pool first dug by the Jin rulers (1115-1234), as well as the artificial island elevated on its surface, and by designing an imperial garden in the northern part of the Palace City. These landscaped areas, which at the time were contained in the imperial city, were transformed during the following dynasties and then served to mark respectively the western and northern perimeter of the Forbidden City (I-28).

It was in this period that Europe first learned of the existence of an Asian tradition of garden art. The first Westerner to speak of it was Marco Polo (1254-1323), the Venetian merchant and traveler who reached China during the reign of Khubilai Kahn. In his account of that adventurous journey, *The Description of the World*, he includes several depictions of great gardens. In describing the parks of what is now Beijing, he noted the presence of wild animals and flora, but also the capacity to construct entire natural landscapes out of nothing. This was what had happened in the area next to the imperial palace, where, with the material excavated in enlarging the artificial body of water called Taiye Lake, a hilly island covered by forest was expanded (I-29). He in fact noted "a hill which has been made by art... This hill is entirely covered with trees that never lose their leaves, but remain ever green. And I assure you that wherever a beautiful tree may exist, and the Emperor gets news of it, he sends for it and has it transported bodily with all its roots and the earth attached to them, and planted on that hill of his. No matter how big the tree may be, he gets it carried by his elephants; and in this way he has got together the most beautiful collection of trees in all the world"[18]. As described by Marco Polo, the imperial gardens of Khubilai Khan had archaic qualities, in their resemblance to the ancient hunting preserves, and also in the name kept for the artificial lake: Taiye Lake was in fact the most famous reflecting pool created by the Han emperors.

I-29

The Gardens of the Ming

The Mongol dynasty of the Yuan was violently replaced by the Chinese Ming dynasty (1368-1644), who governed in a period of a strong nationalistic spirit. Once they had defeated them, the Ming tried to erase all traces of the Mongols on Chinese soil. When the third Ming emperor, Yongle (reigned 1403-1424), transferred the capital definitively from Nanjing to Beijing, the urban and garden works of Khubilai Kahn were largely destroyed, except for the great lake excavated in the western part of the imperial city: and even this was entirely transformed. It was expanded on the south side and divided into three oblong lakes called the Three Seas. Three artificial islands completed the composition, evoking, according to tradition, the mythical dwellings of the Immortals lost in the oceans. Gardens and pavilions were distributed along the shores of the three lakes and the complex, which embraced the western part of the imperial palaces, took the name *Xi yuan*, "West Garden".

The Ming period was marked by a strong centralization of power in the figure of the emperor and by a progressive closure of the empire to outside influences as a way of protecting China from invaders. Political centralization also found expression in urban construction. The work carried out in the area of the Three Seas was only part of an impressive plan to transform Beijing into a great imperial capital (I-30). Using part of the foundations of the Beijing of the Yuan, the Ming built new city walls, palaces, temples and gardens. The design of the new capital followed the classical urban structure of Chinese cities, with its rectangular plan oriented according to the cardinal directions and enclosed within high walls. At the center of the walled rectangle rose the Forbidden City, a city within the city, containing the complex of imperial palaces made up of a progression of great courtyards and buildings set along a central south-north axis.

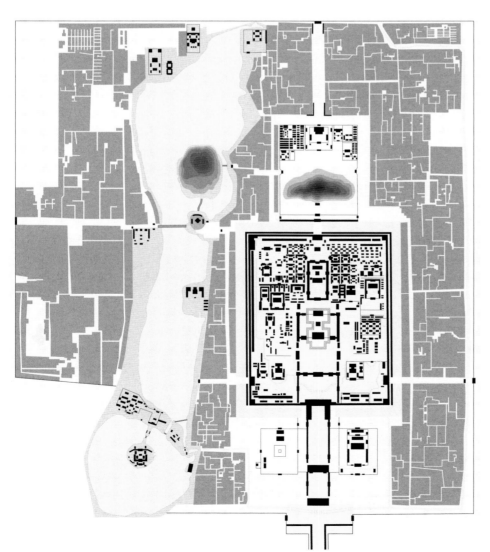

I-30: Map of Beijing during the Qing dynasty, with the Three Seas named Beihai, "Northern Sea", Zhonghai, "Middle Sea", and Nanhai, "Southern Sea".

I-31: Forbidden City, Beijing. The "Golden Water Stream", the artificial channel that meanders through the Forbidden City, is supplied by the moat.

I-32: Forbidden City. With its marble balustrades the "Golden Water Stream" flows through the first paved court between the Meridian Gate and the Gate of Supreme Harmony assuming a bow shape, overpassed by five parallel marble bridges.

I-33: Forbidden City. Four watchtowers are built in correspondence of the corners of the wall, encircled by the moat, encompassing the Forbidden City. A branch canal from the Beihai supplies the moat.

I-34: Beijing. The artificial hill built to the immediate north of the Forbidden City, nowadays a public park called Jingshan Park, is characterized by five peaks, each of which features a pavilion.

The Forbidden City in turn was enclosed within walls surrounded by a wide moat, from which a channel flowed crossing the interior of the complex (I-33). In correspondence with the first court of the Forbidden City, the twisting course of this stream formed a wide arch and was crossed by five richly decorated marble bridges (I-31; I-32). The soil excavated for the moat was used to build an artificial hill, the *Jingshan*, "Coal Hill", that marked the northern perimeter of the Forbidden City[19]. That was the completion of the sequence of natural elements, placed according to the principles of geomancy, which surrounded the Forbidden City: the curve of the stream to the south, the Three Seas to the west, and the hill to the north (I-34).

While the Ming sovereigns were not great builders of new parks, private gardens flourished in all the main cities during their rule; and it was not only the intellectuals and officials who built them. In the second half of the 16th century, China experienced a strong economic expansion, concentrated in its initial phases in the already flourishing region south of the Yangtse River called Jiangnan. It was in this area, and particularly in the cities of Suzhou and Hangzhou, that rich merchants began to make gardens to beautify their urban residences. That favorable situation saw the emergence of the figure of the garden designer, a man at the service of private patrons who, by now, were quite varied. It was in this period, perhaps partly because of the unprecedented creation of private gardens, that the first theoretical work on Chinese garden art appeared. It was a compendium of compositional principles and of planning techniques, published with the title *Yuanye*, *The Craft of Gardens*. This practical three-volume manual, dated 1634, was the work of Ji Cheng (1582-?), a master designer of the age, who suggested diverse general solutions to garden plans in relation to their sites, proposing a big repertory of elements to use in composing the garden's various parts[20].

I-31 ⎯⎯⎯⎯⎯⎯⎯⎯⎯⎯⎯⎯⎯⎯⎯⎯⎯⎯⎯⎯⎯⎯⎯⎯⎯⎯

I-32 ⎯⎯⎯⎯⎯⎯⎯⎯⎯⎯⎯⎯⎯⎯⎯⎯⎯⎯⎯⎯⎯⎯⎯⎯⎯⎯

I-33 ⎯⎯⎯⎯⎯⎯⎯⎯⎯⎯⎯⎯⎯⎯⎯⎯⎯⎯⎯⎯⎯⎯⎯⎯⎯⎯

I-34 ⎯⎯⎯⎯⎯⎯⎯⎯⎯⎯⎯⎯⎯⎯⎯⎯⎯⎯⎯⎯⎯⎯⎯⎯⎯⎯

The Gardens of the Qing

The last imperial dynasty, the Qing (1644-1911), came from Manchuria. Because of this foreign origin, it went to great lenghts to be accepted by the Chinese people, and did not hesitate to follow the taste in design developed under the preceding dynasty. The new parks it created were impressive, as were the private gardens, and the Quing dynasty showed great vivacity in keeping the tradition alive until at least the end of the 18th century.

In this period, garden design developed differently in the north and the south. The cold dry climate of the north, and the limited range of building materials, gave birth to a solid and sober style, especially in Beijing and the surrounding area. The southern gardens, especially in the cities near the Yangtse River – Suzhou, Hangzhou, Yangzhou – were more graceful, open and luminous. The reason can be found in the milder and more humid climate, which enabled luxuriant vegetation and flowering periods that were significantly longer than those of the north. But the differences also concerned the structures in the gardens: southern gardens boasted pavilions with roofs which show a more sweeping curvature rising at the corner of the roof than those in the gardens of the north (I-35; I-36); walls and facades facing the green spaces were pierced by many more doors and windows, in an effort to bring the residential pavilions' indoors and the garden into close relation with each other[21] (I-37).

If private gardens had more modest dimensions than those of the Ming period, because the cities' population was more dense and their area was limited, they were created with compositional techniques that enabled a great variety of visual effects even within limited space. The secret for achieving rich diversity was a series of means to deal with the garden's visual segmentation by offering a sequence of different views.

An admirable example of an articulated composition in a relatively small area is the *Ou yuan*, "Couple's Garden Retreat", in the city of Suzhou (I-38). It occupies 8000 m², and was created in the early Qing period and enlarged in 1874. The garden is divided into two main parts, East and West Garden, separated by the residential quarter. A rockery made of lake stones

I-35: Yihe yuan, "Garden of the Preservation of Harmony", Beijing. Tiled roofs with slightly curved overhanging eaves are characteristic of pavilions in the gardens of northern China.

I-36: Yu yuan, "Garden to Please", Shanghai. Pavilions in the gardens of the southern regions feature roof forms with soaring edges.

I-37: Canglang ting, "Surging Waves Pavilion", Suzhou. The many openings, screens and latticeworks framing the walls of the garden pavilions establish a sense of continuity between indoors and outdoors.

I-38: Ou yuan, "Couple's Garden Retreat", Suzhou. Plan of the garden.

A West Garden
B East Garden

1 Entrance Hall
2 Sedan Chair Hall
3 Carrying Wine Hall
4 Multi-storied Building
5 Library Tower
6 Old House of Woven Courtains
7 Longevity Pavilion
8 Hall of Nobility
9 Hermit Couple's Pillow of the Waves
10 Amongst the Mountains and Water
11 Kuixing Pavilion
12 House of Practicing Daoism
13 My Love Pavilion
14 Moon-viewing Pavilion
15 Ink Slab Returning Studio
16 Thatched Cottage at the City Corner

0   5   10 m

I-36

I-37

I-38

characterizes the West Garden, while the East Garden is articulated around an elongated pond, dominated by an artificial yellow granite mountain. The pond is crossed by a zigzag bridge and bordered by rocks and pavilions (I-39; I-40).

In the course of the 18th century, the urban gardens of Suzhou, as well as the natural landscapes near the lower Yangtse River, served as inspiration for the design of the big imperial parks. Through the evocation, and sometimes the deliberate replica, of certain famous places of southern China, the Qing sovereigns tried to recreate the atmosphere of the south in their suburban parks near Beijing[22].

It was during the reign of three consecutive emperors of this dynasty, Kangxi (reigned 1662-1722), Yongzheng (reigned 1723-1735) and Qianlong (reigned 1736-1795), that the art of the garden in China knew its richest era. The emperors distinguished themselves in commissioning parks, and their summer residences near the capital became the privileged realm of experimental compositions (I-41).

The residence of *Bishu shanzhuang*, "Mountain Hamlet to Escape the Summer Heat", was built in a mountainous area northeast of Beijing, near the city of Chengde (I-42). The park was begun in 1703, during the reign of the Kangxi Emperor, and its construction lasted for nearly the whole century. The site was a valley with many wooded undulations. In its southern part, the valley opened into a flat area where the imperial palaces were built. On a reduced scale, these were modeled on the Forbidden City, with a sequence of courts. Behind the more private area, toward the north, a great natural-looking lake was excavated, its surface punctuated by numerous islands linked by bridges. Pavilions, temples and other structures of varying functions were sprinkled around the lake and on the heights enclosing the park (I-43).

A few years later, in 1709, on a plain rich with water sources northwest of the walls of Beijing, construction began of what would become the *Yuanming yuan*, "Garden of Perfect Brightness". This vast property covered about 300 ha; it underwent continual expansion during the century, and was later destroyed in 1860 in the course of a military campaign conducted by Anglo-French troops, linked to the request for greater trading privileges. It was composed

I-39: Ou yuan, "Couple's Garden Retreat", Suzhou. Rocky composition in the western section of the garden.

I-40: Ou yuan. A pond, crossed by a zigzag bridge, stretches on the eastern section of the garden.

I-41: Anonymous court artist, *The Qianlong Emperor Watching Peacocks Displaying Tails*. Qing dynasty. Ink and color on silk, 340 x 537 cm.

I-42: Leng Mei, *The Summer Resort in Chengde*. Qing dynasty. Hanging scroll, color on silk, 254.8 x 172.5 cm

I-43: Bishu shanzhuang, "Mountain Hamlet to Escape the Summer Heat", Chengde. Plan of the park.

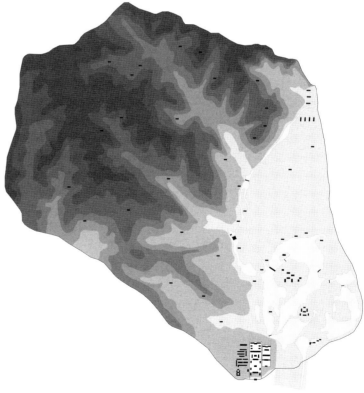

⊕ 0 100 500 m

I-41

I-42

I-43

of three distinct gardens, independent from each other but connected: *Changchun yuan*, "Garden of Everlasting Spring", *Qichun yuan*, "Garden of Ten Thousand Springs", and *Yuan-ming yuan*. This last one was the biggest and gave its name to the whole complex (I-44). While the *Bishu shanzhuang* was dominated by mountainous heights, the diverse parts of the *Yuanming yuan* were linked by a water network. The three gardens, visually separated by artificial hills, were organized around lakes of varying dimensions, connected by canals of serpentine shape. The whole complex included hills, valleys, rock formations and it contained a number of palaces, pavilions and small gardens inserted in larger green spaces, making for ever-changing scenic spots. Because of its vast dimension, compositional complexity, and function in representing imperial dignity, the European Jesuits who visited *Yuanming yuan* in the 18th century did not hesitate to call it the "Versailles of China", experiencing it as comparable only to that noblest and most impressive park ensemble in Europe[23].

I-44: Tang Dai and Shen Yuan, *Forty Views of Yuanmingyuan*, 1747. Vol. 1, scene 8, *Shangxia tianguang*, "Celestial clarity in the sky and down here". Ink and watercolor on silk.

I-45: Xihu, "West Lake", Hangzhou. One of the causeways crossing the West Lake. The peculiar morphology of the site was one of the sources of inspiration for the enlargement of the Yihe yuan imperial park in Beijing.

I-46: Yihe yuan, "Garden of the Preservation of Harmony", Beijing. Plan of the park.

I-47: Yihe yuan. The park is designed as a juxtaposition of the steep Longevity Hill and the large Kunming Lake, which stretches out in front of the hill, occupying three quarters of the whole park.

I-48: Yihe yuan. The South Lake Island is connected by the marble "Seventeen-Arch Bridge".

I-49: Yihe yuan. The "Suzhou Street", where two rows of shops are lined up along the banks, was designed as an evocation of the canals of Suzhou.

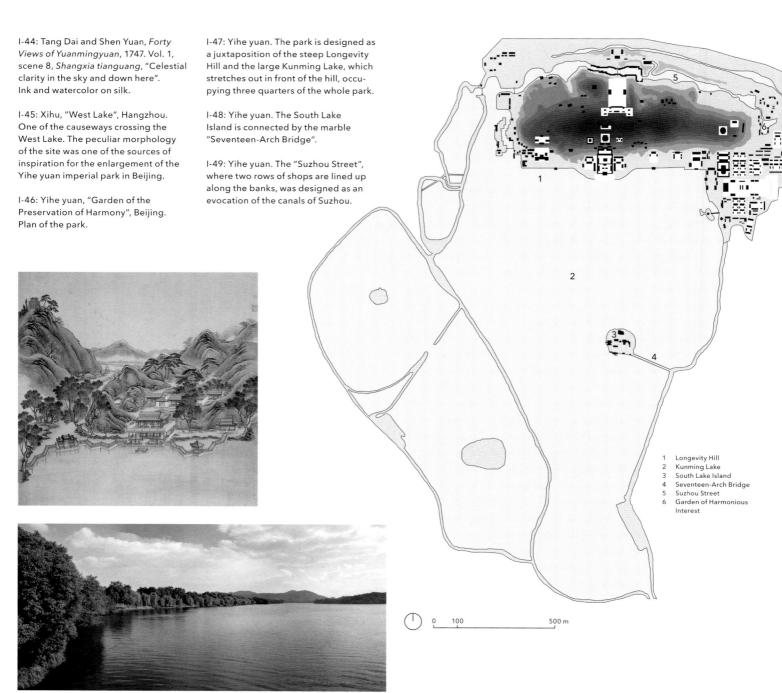

1   Longevity Hill
2   Kunming Lake
3   South Lake Island
4   Seventeen-Arch Bridge
5   Suzhou Street
6   Garden of Harmonious Interest

0   100   500 m

I-44
I-45
I-46

The Qianlong Emperor was a true collector of landscapes; in 1771 he ordered from Suzhou a model of a garden from that city, called *Shizi lin*, "Lion Grove", celebrated for rock compositions that made it resemble a petrified forest. On the basis of that model, he had two replicas created: one within the garden of *Changchun yuan* and the other in the summer residence of Chengde[24]. Yet the practice of constructing scenes which evoke famous natural or man-made landscapes, within the perimeter of parks and gardens would reach far greater results. This happened in a third summer residence of the Qing period, the *Qingyi yuan*, "Garden of Clear Ripples", in which the whole general composition was inspired by the natural landscape of the *Xihu*, "West Lake", a big lake surrounded by high hills on three sides west of the city of Hangzhou (I-45). Built between 1750 and 1764 west of the *Yuanming yuan*, this later imperial park was twice damaged by Western troops. On both occasions it was rebuilt by the Empress Dowager Cixi (1835-1908) and it was after the first reconstruction that it took its present name: *Yihe yuan*, "Garden of the Preservation of Harmony" (I-46). The design of the 300-ha park is centered on the harmonious composition of an elevated crest and a great lake, both artificial. The hill, named *Wanshou shan*, "Longevity Hill", occupies the northern part of the site; covered by thick woods, it is graced by temples, pavilions and gardens spread over the hill's irregular slopes, connected by winding paths. At the foot of the hill, the big lake opens toward the south, inspired by the West Lake of Hangzhou (I-47). This body of water, which following the imperial tradition bears as well the name Kunming Lake, is the principal element of the composition, occupying three quarters of the surface of the park. A perfectly circular artificial island, connected to the shore by a long marble bridge, was created in the southern part of the lake (I-48). In its northwestern part, the Kunming Lake narrows into a channel and it is along this watercourse that another famous place is evoked, neither a garden nor a natural landscape but a piece of a city: the canals of Suzhou and the intense commercial activity conducted along their quays. This is Suzhou Street, with its rows of low buildings which once housed shops facing the canals. When the Qianlong Emperor had them built, they made up a living microcosm imitating an urban trading quarter, an occasion of amusement for the imperial court[25] (I-49).

I-47

I-48

I-49

The Chinese Garden in Modern Times

The two reconstructions of the park of *Yihe yuan* commissioned by the Empress Dowager Cixi represent the last green bulwark of imperial power in a period of great political turmoil. It seems that in order to pay for the first reconstruction, which was executed in 1888, Cixi used funds allocated for the expansion of the fleet; the empress saw the reconstruction of the park as a more effective signal for affirming the imperial supremacy than an improvement of the navy could have been. And the second reconstruction, stubbornly carried out in 1903, was intended by the empress dowager as a powerful symbolic act, an extreme attempt to demonstrate the imperial family's capacity to face internal chaos and foreign challenges, while casting a veil on the dynasty's decline (I-50). The imperial gardens over time had become the persistent emblem of the Chinese empire itself, and the reconstruction of *Yihe yuan,* epic or pathetic as one may perceive it, offers a paradigmatic example of an archaic world's resistance to the forced and violent modernization to which the country was to be submitted in the 20th century.

When the Republic of China was established in 1912, the last Qing emperor, Puyi, titled the Xuantong Emperor (1906-1967; reigned 1909-1911), was deposed and confined to the northern part of the Forbidden City. That at least guaranteed the survival of the imperial gardens within the perimeter of the complex[26] and also of the summer residence of *Yihe yuan,* which until 1924 remained the main scene of the life of Puyi and his court. Meanwhile, the President of the new Republic settled down in the area of the Three Seas, west of the Forbidden City, where his residence and government offices were placed in the southern part of the park; from that moment, these areas were separated from the northernmost lake, *Beihai,* which together with the surrounding green area subsequently became a public park (I-51). Other imperial parks were transformed into public parks. This happened in Beijing with the Altar of Land and Grain, a sacred space where the emperors had offered sacrifices to the divinities of the earth and of agriculture, located southwest of the Forbidden City. In 1914 this space became a public park with the name "Central Park" (now Zhongshan Park); the name itself, adopted from New York's park, showed that modernization was inherent to its transformation.

I-50: Yihe yuan, "Garden of the Preservation of Harmony", Beijing. The southern slope of the Longevity Hill overlooking the Kunming Lake.

I-51: Beihai Park, Beijing. Plan of the park.

I-52: Beihai Park. One of the two bridges which connect the Qionghua Island with the park.

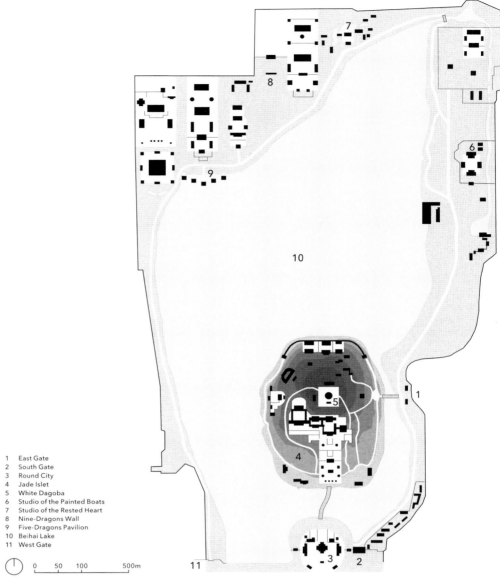

1 East Gate
2 South Gate
3 Round City
4 Jade Islet
5 White Dagoba
6 Studio of the Painted Boats
7 Studio of the Rested Heart
8 Nine-Dragons Wall
9 Five-Dragons Pavilion
10 Beihai Lake
11 West Gate

0   50   100   500m

I-51

Many gardens belonging to the imperial family, also some green spaces connected to temples or in private use, fell progressively into a state of abandonment in the long period of disorder – the internal strife among warlords, civil war, and the Japanese invasion – which shook China in the first half of the 20th century. After the establishment in 1949 of the People's Republic of China under Mao Zedong, the few newly created parks and gardens had a mainly utilitarian character and were rigid and monumental in design. No longer considered as a cultural patrimony, some historical gardens were destroyed between 1966 and 1976 during the Cultural Revolution; some were saved only because they were occupied by government offices or by important members of the Communist Party.

It was only around the 1980s that the historical tradition of the gardens began to be appreciated and studied, and was recognized as a powerful contribution to the Chinese cultural identity[27]. A symbol of this renewed interest is the small garden around the Hong Kong headquarters of the Bank of China, designed starting from 1982 by the New York-based Sino-American architect I. M. Pei (I-53). The bank's steel and glass tower is complemented by a garden of rocks and water which, integrating the geometry of triangular lines that shapes the profile of the jagged tower, reinterprets the traditional stylistic elements in entirely new forms (I-54; I-55).

When on August 8, 2008, the opening ceremony for the Olympics took place in Beijing, the stadium built for the occasion by Swiss architects Jacques Herzog and Pierre de Meuron, with the participation of Chinese artist and architect Ai Weiwei, was transformed into a global stage for Chinese history and culture. The succession of choreographic scenes recounting the salient events in China's long history had a precise meaning: it demonstrated how China had decided to reaffirm its own identity in the global context, with the weight of its extraordinary history and the permanence of its cultural heredity. Outside the stadium, the Olympic Green (2003-2008) underlines the principle of continuity between past and present in the name of a Chinese tradition stirred into the global cauldron (I-56). The Olympic Green, designed on the basis of a masterplan first developed by Sasaki Associates, consists of the Olympic Central Area, the new urban park alongside the Olympic

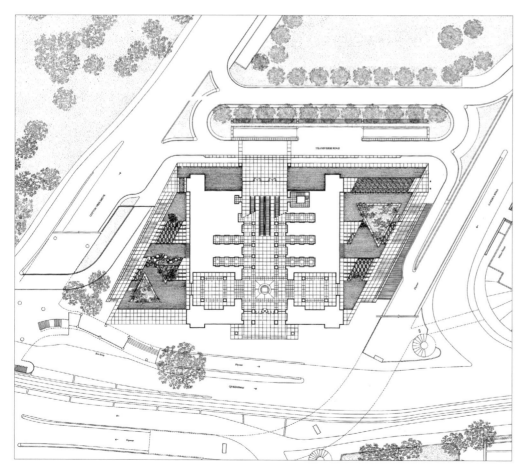

I-53: Bank of China, Hong Kong. Plan of the bank tower and the surrounding garden, completed in 1989.

I-54: Bank of China. The rock and water garden combines modern language and traditional elements.

I-55: Bank of China. The garden responds to the sloping site with a system of little waterfalls supplying various pools at different levels.

I-56: Olympic Green, Beijing. The Bird's Nest designed by Jacques Herzog and Pierre de Meuron acts as a distinctive landmark for the southern part of the park system.

I-53

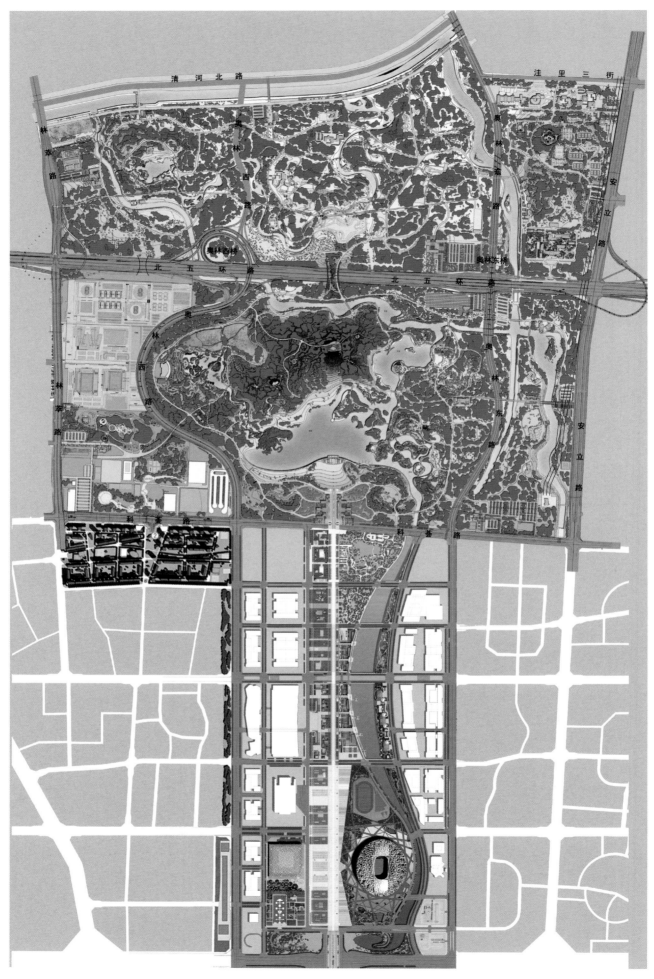

Evolution and Typology

venues, and the Olympic Forest Park; the latter, designed by a team led by landscape architect Hu Jie, closes the Olympic area to the north[28] (I-57). The very position of the two parks in the urban structure of Beijing expresses a wish to connect to the past: the Olympic Central Area, a park of linear form, constitutes the prolongation northward of the central axis of the Forbidden City (I-58). Thus it extends the spine along which the imperial capital has been organized since the era of the Yuan, connecting the past glories of China in the Forbidden City with the ones hoped for for the future, represented by the Olympic site[29]. The Olympic Forest Park, with its artificial hills, concludes this axis northward in a design gesture so often used in Chinese parks, that of using heights and vegetation to protect them against the north, considered inauspicious in geomancy[30] (I-59).

Within the two parks as well, the Chinese garden tradition has been fully exploited. The Olympic Green is organized around a winding stream which falls northward into a lake at the center of the Olympic Forest Park, whose jagged edge evokes the head of a dragon (I-60). Behind the lake there is an artificial hill, whose rocky slopes echo the imperial parks of the Qing dynasty. In a semantic operation almost cartoon-like in its immediacy, the strong and long-shared metaphor of imperial China, the dragon, takes its place at the heart of the composition to evoke the link with the past, while water, rocks, artificial hills and rice paddies interpret the landscape tradition in new compositional forms, continuing that infinite investigation into the meaning and essence of naturalness which first engendered the Chinese Garden (I-61).

I-57: Olympic Green, Beijing. Masterplan, with both the Olympic Central Area and the Olympic Forest Park. The park system was completed in 2008.

I-58: Olympic Central Area, Beijing. Organized around a winding stream, the Olympic Central Area is a linear park alongside the sports facilities built for the 2008 Olympic Games.

I-59: Olympic Forest Park, Beijing. Artificial earthworks created using soil excavated from the construction sites define a hilly curtain in the northern part of the park.

I-60: Olympic Forest Park. The park concludes northward the central axis around which the city of Beijing developed historically.

I-61: Olympic Forest Park. A constructed wetland is part of a sophisticated self-sustaining and self-regulating water system.

I-58 ——————————————————————— I-59 ———————————————————————

I-60 ——— I-61 ———————

I-62: Shanghai Houtan Park. Completed in 2010, the park is organized around a constructed wetland, designed to create a new ecological water treatment and flood control system.

I-63: Shanghai Houtan Park. Reclaimed industrial materials, forming small structures offering shade and shelter, are inserted in the matrix of an ecologically regenerated landscape.

I-64: Shanghai Houtan Park. Structures conveying memories of the industrial past have remained on site and have been transformed to accommodate new functions, like the Hanging Garden.

I-65

I-63

I-64

Functions and Use

In recent years, China has created many completely new public parks. The largest of these were designed on the occasion of grand events which provoked the reconfiguration of entire urban areas and were intended to represent contemporary China to the world: this is the case of the Olympic Green in Beijing made for the 2008 Olympics, or of the Shanghai Houtan Park in Shanghai (2007-2010), created since 2007 as part of the Expo 2010 by land-scape architect Kongjian Yu, founder of the Beijing-based firm Turenscape (I-62). This lat-ter park features walking paths through rich and diverse flora, open spaces for leisure and socializing, more intimate and isolated areas for tranquil recreation and solitary repose. But this functional design, aimed at enhancing the visitor's well-being, is integrated with compositional features soliciting memory and imagination. The park stretches on a for-mer industrial area once occupied by a steel factory and a shipyard along the Huangpu River. The recovery of this degraded space was through a regenerative design strategy, with transformation of the site into a living system that offers comprehensive ecological services, like food production and water treatment (I-63).

This park is thus a wetland that can be traversed by the public, with integration of frag-ments of the agricultural landscape that once existed alongside the river as well as of its industrial past, all in a context denoting the future of our post-industrial eco-civilization. With its educational purpose, its aesthetic form, the park intends to present a synthesis of the cultural and natural memory of the place (I-64).

Integrating thus recreational and representational functions with visual and intellectual stimuli, mixing spaces for physical activity and for appreciating nature with reminiscences of the terrain's past, China's new public parks offer a compendium of uses that Chinese Gardens have fulfilled historically.

The representational function appeared as central from the origins onwards, since the first parks we have knowledge of, those of rulers of the earliest dynasties, were essentially vast properties with woods and lakes, fenced in mainly for hunting purposes, but also for conducting the propitiatory rites reserved as part of the imperial function, linked to agri-cultural practices.

With consolidation of centralized power, the imperial parks' value in representing that power increased: they became the scene of court rituals and of state affairs. Paintings commissioned by the sovereigns and replicated in multiple series, as well as poems some-times written by the emperors themselves, made known the grandiose forms of these sophisticated green architectures and underlined their celebratory role. These were the places where ambassadors and foreign delegations were received. In 1793, the English diplomatic mission led by Lord Macartney was received successively at Chengde, in the residence of *Bishu shanzhuang*, and in the residence of *Yuanming yuan*. The Empress Dowager Cixi invited the wives of the Western ambassadors in Beijing to her summer residence of *Yihe yuan*.

Replicating on a small scale the role of imperial gardens, private gardens as well were understood as spaces for refined exhibition of the economic status and social level reached by the owner, where friends could be entertained informally while banquets, feasts and musical events could be held as well. This was particularly evident after the 16th cen-tury, as purely aesthetic interest in the forms of gardens and social activities in gardens increased. The gardens of the literati and high state officials in the Ming period became more and more theaters of cultivated competition in matters of taste; spaces for entertain-ing acquaintances and building social relations. Entertaining and leisure activities were not lacking also in imperial gardens, which served for the amusement of the court, and they were the scene of parties and games. Sports were not lacking either; while *cuju*, the Chi-nese soccer reserved to nobles, was practiced from the Han period, the Tang dynasty saw the rise of *jiju* or polo, perhaps imported from India.

The habit of opening private gardens to visitors is ancient; in the Song period, the peony gardens of Luoyang and like other private aristocratic gardens were open to the public at least for certain periods, as were other urban gardens. In the Ming period some imperial gardens and the gardens of the hereditary imperial aristocracy were opened to visitors as well[31]. But Chinese Gardens were also appreciated as private retreats, as they offered a place for solitary meditation. The private gardens often created by high officials who had retired from public life were spaces of a more reserved character, destined above all to contemplation and study. Historical descriptions tended to consider these gardens, often located within cities, as a sort of refuge, at least momentarily isolating their owners from worldly concerns, enabling them to find anew the equanimity to face life beyond the garden's walls.

Private gardens were, at least in part and in certain periods, productive resources. The cultivated withdrawal from public life, the Confucian ideal of auto-sufficiency and the search for ancient simplicity did not exclude the possibility that aesthetic enjoyment might be accompanied by economic return on agronomical production. Many green spaces helped enrich the table and improve the financial situation of their owners, and in some cases acquired a mainly utilitarian character. In the Song period, the city of Luoyang was famous for the production of ornamental plants and above all of peonies, which were cultivated in special gardens by horticulturalists and sold all over China. The official Sima Guang (1019-1086) preferred in his *Dule yuan*, "Garden of Solitary Enjoyment", located in the ancient capital of Luoyang, medicinal plants to ornamental ones: their sale also was a source of income, since they played a fundamental role in Chinese pharmaceuticals. The garden thus constituted a sort of autarkic landscape: it offered its owner quiet and prestige; it also produced products useful in daily life of the household; then too it guaranteed an income, because those same products were sold in city markets[32]. The presence of utilitarian cultivation in the garden was recorded in the Ming period as well. The *Zhuozheng yuan*, "Garden of the Humble Administrator", was created in Suzhou in the first decades of the 16th century and often altered since. The original composition of his garden, long since lost, included a substantial number of useful plants including fruit trees, cypresses and junipers, as well as medicinal herbs, and in the garden's reflecting pools fish were raised[33]. After the 16th century, that productive function diminished.

A renewal of the idea of the garden as a productive site can be recognized in some contemporary landscape architecture projects. Inspired by Chinese agricultural landscape, its fields and plantings, they rediscover the aesthetic quality of horticulture (I-65).

I-62: Shanghai Houtan Park, Shanghai. The park features terraces planted with native crops which recall Shanghai's agricultural landscape.

Evolution and Typology

1: Cibot writes: "The great art of these gardens is to copy nature in all her simplicity, to avoid her disorder, and to hide under the veil of her irregularity." Pierre-Marital Cibot, "Essai sur les Jardins de plaisance des Chinois", in *Mémoires concernant l'histoire, les sciences, les arts, les mœurs, les usages, & c., des Chinois: par les Missionnaires de Pékin*, vol. VIII (Paris: Nyon, 1782), 318. Translation by the author.

2: Pierre-Martial Cibot, "Le Jardin de Sée-Ma-Kouang," in *Mémoires*, vol. II (Paris: Nyon, 1777), 643. Translation by the author.

3: Cibot, "Essai", 318. Translation by the author.

4: George Macartney, *An Embassy to China: being the Journal Kept by Lord Macartney during His Embassy to the Emperor Ch'ien-Lung, 1793-1794*, ed. J. L. Cranmer-Byng (London: Longmans, 1962), 271.

5: These were the words used by Chen Congzhou, a great Chinese expert in the field, to characterize Chinese Gardens, as recorded in Hui Zhou, "The *jing* of a perspective garden", *Studies in the History of Gardens & Designed Landscapes* 22, 4 (2002): 326, note 139.

6: See Hu Dongchu, *The Way of the Virtuous. The Influence of Art and Philosophy on Chinese Garden Design* (Beijing: New World Press, 1991).

7: For an historical survey of these compounds see Edward H. Schafer, "Hunting Parks and Animal Enclosures in Ancient China", *Journal of the Economic and Social History of the Orient* 11, 3 (Oct. 1968): 318-43. Among the relevant literature offering a general reconstruction of the historical evolution of Chinese Gardens see Norah Titley and Frances Wood, *Oriental Gardens* (London: British Library, 1991), 70-98; Peter Valder, *Gardens in China* (Portland, OR: Timber Press, 2002); Maggie Keswick, *The Chinese Garden* (London: Frances Lincoln, 2003²); Che Bing Chiu, *Jardins de Chine ou la quête du paradis* (Paris: Édition de La Martinière, 2010); Xiaofeng Fang, *The Great Gardens of China* (New York: Monacelli Press, 2010).

8: In the course of time, stretches of the original Grand Canal decayed. The actual length of the Grand Canal is accepted to be 1,794 km. For the Grand Canal see Joseph Needham, *Science and Civilization in China: Volume IV, Physics and Physical Technology, Part 3, Civil Engineering and Nautics* (Cambridge: Cambridge University Press, 1971), 306-19; see also John Keay, *China. A History* (London: Harper Press, 2008), 230-32.

9: See Xiaoshan Yang, "Li Deyu's Pingquan Villa: Forming an Emblem from the Tang to the Song", *Asia Maior* 17, 2 (2004): 45-88.

10: The dynasty of the Song is divided chronologically into two periods: the Northern Song, with its capital at Bianliang, and the Southern Song (1127-1279) with its capital at Lin'an (present-day Hangzhou). Following the Jurchen invasion of the central-northern regions of China and the seizure of Bianliang in 1127, the court took refuge in the south of the country, thus beginning the Southern Song dynasty. The Jurchen established the Jin dynasty in the north of the country and were defeated in 1234 by the Mongols. See Keay, *China*, 327-50.

11: For a study of the *Genyue*, see James M. Hargett, "Huizong's Magic Marchmount: the Genyue Pleasure Park of Kaifeng", *Monumenta Serica* 38 (1988-1989): 1-48.

12: Quoted in Li Gefei, "Famous Gardens of Luoyang", ed. and trans. Philip Watson, *Studies in the History of Gardens & Designed Landscape* 24, 1 (2004): 42.

13: Quoted in *Ibid.*, 42.

14: Quoted in *Ibid.*, 47.

15: Quoted in Georges Métailié, "Gardens of Luoyang: The Refinements of a City Culture", in *Gardens, City Life and Culture: A World Tour*, ed. Michel Conan and Chen Wangheng (Cambridge, MA: Harvard University Press, 2008), 32.

16: On *Canglang ting*'s history and the modifications of the garden through time, see Xu Yinong, "Interplay of Image and Fact: the Pavilion of Surging Waves, Suzhou", *Studies in the History of Gardens & Designed Landscapes, Chinese Gardens II* 19, 3/4 (1999): 288-301.

17: On Dadu, capital city of the Yuan dynasty, see Nancy S. Steinhardt, *Chinese Imperial City Planning* (Honolulu, HI: University of Hawaii Press, 1990), 154-60. For an historical excursus on the evolution of Beijing from the origin to recent years see Claudio Greco and Carlo Santoro, *Beijing. The new city* (Milano: Skira, 2008). See also Peter G. Rowe, *East Asia Modern. Shaping the contemporary city* (London: Reaktion Books, 2005).

18: In: Marco Polo, *The Book of Ser Marco Polo, the Venetian, concerning the Kingdoms and Marvels of the East*, trans. and ed. Henry Yule and Henri Cordier, vol. I (St. Helier: Armorica Book, 1975³), 365.

19: For a discussion of Beijing in the Ming and Qing periods, see: Steinhardt, *Chinese Imperial City Planning*, 169-78. On the construction of the Forbidden City and its changes in the Ming and Qing periods see Frances Wood, "Imperial Architecture of the Qing: Palaces and Retreats", in *China. The Three Emperors, 1662-1795*, ed. Evelyn S. Rawski and Jessica Rawson (London: Royal Academy of Arts, 2005), 54-60.

20: Ji Cheng's manual filled three volumes. The first contains general principles: evaluation of the site, general composition and garden architectures; the second deal with balustrades; the third volume is dedicated to doors and windows, pavements and external walls, and includes a study on how to create artificial mountains, as well as on the choice of stones for gardens, with indications of where to find them. The last chapter of the third volume focuses on how to compose the various scenes and their sequence inside the garden. For Ji Cheng and *Yuanye* see the bibliography.

21: See Sun Dazhang, "The Qing Dynasty", in *Chinese Architecture*, ed. Nancy S. Steinhardt (New Haven, Conn.: Yale University Press, 2002), 297-98.

22: See Jia Jun, "Les Jardins du Jiangnan dans l'art paysager à Pékin, pendant les Ming et Qing", in Gilles Baud-Berthier, Sophie Couëtoux and Che Bing Chiu, *Le Jardin du lettré: Synthèse des arts en Chine* (Besançon: Les Éditions de l'Imprimeur, 2004), 173.

23: The comparison can be found in: Jean-Denis Attiret, "Lettre du frère Attiret de la Compagnie de Jésus, peintre au service de l'empereur de Chine, à M. D'Assaut, Pékin, le 1er novembre 1743", in *Lettres édifiantes et curieuses, écrites des missions étrangères, par quelques Missionnaires de la Compagnie de Jésus*, vol. XXVII (Paris: Guerin, 1749), 43; in Pierre-Martial Cibot, "Notices de quelques Plantes, Arbriesseaux, etc. de la Chine," in *Mémoires*, vol. III (Paris: Nyon, 1778), 443. For a recent comparison between Versailles and the *Yuanming yuan* see: Greg M. Thomas, "Yuanming Yuan/Versailles: Intercultural Interaction Between Chinese and European Palace Cultures," *Art History* 32, 1 (2009): 115-43. On the Jesuits' descriptions of Chinese gardens see: Bianca Maria Rinaldi, *The 'Chinese Garden in Good Taste'. Jesuits and Europe's Knowledge of Chinese Flora and Art of the Garden in 17th and 18th Centuries* (Munich: Meidenbauer, 2006), chapter 6.

24: See Jia, "Les Jardins", 175-76.

25: A similar but much bigger quarter, almost a miniature city, must have existed also within the imperial park of *Yuanming yuan*. The French Jesuit Jean-Denis Attiret offered a description in a famous letter sent from Beijing in 1743. The miniature city in the *Yuanming yuan* was a lively animated place set up by eunuchs for the emperor and his court, where games and spectacles were staged in an urban setting of festive confusion. See Attiret, "Lettre", 22-29.

26: The *Yuhua yuan*, the imperial garden north of the imperial palaces, and the Qianlong garden in the complex of the *Ningshou gong*, "Palace of Tranquil Longevity", are in the northeastern quadrant of the Forbidden City, built in 1689 and enlarged by the Qianlong Emperor from 1771 onwards; this is where he withdrew after his abdication in 1795.

27: The work by the pioneering Chinese architectural historian Liu Dunzhen, *Suzhou gudian yuanlin* [Classical Gardens of Suzhou], considered of primary importance for the theoretical research about the traditional garden in China, was published in 1979.

28: In 2002 the US-American interdisciplinary design and planning firm Sasaki Associates Inc. won the commission for the masterplan for the Olympic Green through an invited, international design competition. The masterplan (2003) was further developed in collaboration with the Beijing Tsinghua Urban Planning and Design Institute, Tsinghua University (Beijing). From 2004 to 2005 a large team led by chief designer Hu Jie, director of the Planning and Design Branch of Landscape Architecture, Beijing Tsinghua Urban Planning and Design Institute, Tsinghua University (Beijing), finished the implementation of the Olympic Forest Park. The project, completed in 2008, was in collaboration with: China Research Center of Landscape Architecture Design and Planning (Beijing), Top Sense Landscape Design Co. Ltd. (Beijing), Beijing Beilin Landscape Architecture Institute Co. Ltd., Beijing Institute of Landscape and Traditional Architecture Design and Research, Beijing Zhongyuan Engineering Design & Consulting Co. and China Urban Construction Design & Research Institute (Beijing). The Olympic Central Area was designed by a team comprising the following companies and institutions: Beijing Institute of Architectural Design, Beijing General Municipal Engineering Design & Research Institute, China Research Center of Landscape Architecture Design and Planning Ç(Beijing), Beijing Institute of Water, Beijing Urban Engineering Design & Research Institute Co. Ltd.

29: For a discussion of the urban interventions connected with the Olympics see Malte Selugga, "The Dragon's Tail", *Topos* 63 (2008): 15-21.

30: See Iris Belle, "Beijing Olympic Forest Park. The Axis to Nature", *Topos* 63 (2008): 25.

31: Craig Clunas, *Fruitful Sites. Garden Culture in Ming Dynasty China* (London: Reaktion Books, 1996), 94-95.

32: Georges Métailié, "Some hints on 'Scholar Gardens' and plants in traditional China", *Studies in the History of Gardens & Designed Landscapes* 18, 3 (1998): 250. On the utilitarian aspect of gardens see also Clunas, *Fruitful Sites*.

33: Clunas, *Fruitful Sites*, 22-59.

Fengshui

In the Chinese Garden the general principles of garden design, such as what is the garden's correct position in relation to the buildings, are strongly influenced by the practice of geomancy, a group of concepts which originated in ancient China to explain natural phenomena and even existence itself. This has been known in more recent centuries as *fengshui*, "wind and water". Geomancy is an amalgam of mystical philosophy, superstition, common sense and aesthetic ideas, inspired by the principle that a harmonious environment favors not only a serene life, but a fortunate one. It is based on the conviction that the environment is permeated by a vital energy, a cosmic breath called *qi*, a dynamic positive or negative life force which moves through the earth following the features of the environment: the conformation of valleys, rivers, mountains, the slope of the land, vegetation, soil quality and its interaction with man-made structures.

The currents of auspicious *qi*, which flow as directed by natural morphology, are considered capable of influencing the fortunes of individuals, and therefore, it is necessary to find the correct location and orientation for all of their earthly places, for life and beyond. Whether it is a city, a house or a tomb, all human structures must be situated in harmony with the earth's breathing, taking advantage of the beneficial influences and avoiding the negative ones called *sha*, which have their origin in an incorrect flow of *qi*[2].

Every transformation of the landscape, every man-made construction, influences the flow of *qi*, and consequently a series of rules were developed, still obeyed today, to guide construction activity, be it building or landscape construction.

The basic rule is that buildings must be oriented toward the south, but their positioning in relation to topography is also of vital importance: sites considered particularly fortunate are those in flat areas, open to the south but protected from the unfortunate winds of the north by hills and mountains, and surrounded by low elevations on the other sides. The terrain must be dry, but crossed by a winding stream flowing preferably from northwest toward southeast[3].

In former times, the choice of a site and the planning of a city, as that of a garden or park, were guided by the principles of *fengshui*. Before construction began, a geomancer was consulted. He checked the site and its water resources, which symbolized well-being and good fortune, and then indicated the correct orientation. In the case of gardens, he defined the position of the green space in relation to the main buildings and the placement of its different elements[4].

In the case that the chosen site, even though considered propitious, did not fully offer the desired characteristics, it was an option to intervene and significantly alter the conformation of the place. Thus, according to the topographical principles, a wooded hill called *Jingshan*, now the central element of Beijing's *Jingshan* Park, the imperial park opposite the north gate of the Forbidden City, was artificially created to protect the imperial palaces and the Forbidden City against evil influences coming from the north. Likewise, the designers of the recent Olympic Forest Park in Beijing created *Yangshan* Mountain, which protects the southern side of the park and, by extension, the whole metropolis (II-10)[5].

In the creation of the imperial park of *Yuanming yuan,* it was the natural water system which underwent the heavy modifications dictated by a geomancer. The springs in the southwestern part of the garden were deviated and moved northwest, so that the water flowed into the imperial park from the north and flowed out to the southeast, in conformity with geomantic principles[6].

II-8: Wangshi yuan, "Garden of the Master of the Fishing Nets", Suzhou. A stone bridge designed according to *fengshui* principles twists over water.

II-9: Zhuozheng yuan, "Garden of the Humble Administrator", Suzhou. Leaving the main path, a zigzagging bridge leads to an island-pavilion.

II-10: The Forbidden City and the Olympic Forest Park are placed along the same ideal south-north axis. Following the *fengshui* principles, both complexes have been protected by an artificial hill on the northern quadrant.

II-11: Shizi lin, "Lion Grove', Suzhou. The water system has its outlet in a smaller pool located in the southeastern quadrant.

II-12: Shizi lin. The waterfall situated in the northwestern quadrant supplies the garden's water system.

II-13: Yihe yuan, "Garden of the Preservation of Harmony", Beijing. Random planted trees hamper the inauspicious influences.

II-14: Shizi lin. The reflecting pool around which the garden is organized. According to *fengshui*, water was considered accumulating beneficial energies.

II-15: Bank of China, Hong Kong. In front of the main entry into the lobby of the Bank of China Tower the garden design features a goldfish pond.

II-16: Bank of China. The rock-and-water garden embracing the tower was designed according to *fengshui* principles.

II-11 ———————————————————————————— II-12 ——————————

II-13 ———————————————————— II-14 ——————————

On another scale, the garden was an important annex to a residence, because thanks to its components water, rocks, hills and trees, it was able to correct any defects of the site and improve its potential. When deemed necessary, the planner introduced artificial earth and rock hillocks or wooded groves to screen the unlucky quadrants; he then indicated the most appropriate arrangement of the waters that were to flow slowly through the garden. This procedure was followed in the *Shizi lin*, "Lion Forest", a garden originally created in the first half of the 14th century in Suzhou, where a waterfall located in the northwestern quadrant feeds a series of pools which ring the entire green space and then find their outlet southeast (II-11; II-12).

Since it was believed that inauspicious influences, *sha*, ran in a straight direction, twisting paths imitating the lines of the natural landscape were preferred. When it was not possible to avoid creating areas whose position entailed the flow of unfavorable influences, their defects were mitigated by a series of devices. The *sha* could in fact be blocked or deviated by walls, groups of rocks or trees arranged in an irregular manner (II-13). And the planners were able to contribute to that the positive flows, once they were collected, would not be dispersed: thus the gardens always had perimeter walls and presented internal divisions as well – walls pierced by narrow doorways – whose task was to conserve the positive vital spirits generated by the passage of the *qi*. Similarly, pools of water were considered points where the *qi*'s beneficial energies accumulated, and this was one of the reasons why they were given a central position in the garden (II-14).

The rules of geomancy continue to guide the orientation of large building complexes and the composition of many green open spaces. When I. M. Pei designed the Bank of China Tower, it was decided that despite the modest size of the lot, good business would be propitiated if three of its sides were occupied by a water garden opening into a basin with gold carps on the southern side of the building, in front of the main entry into the lobby (II-15). The garden design is entirely modern despite its inspiration by the ancient practice of geomancy (II-16). On a bigger scale, an emblematic contemporary example is the new Botanical Garden of Chenshan near Shanghai, designed by a group led by the German landscape architects Donata and Christoph Valentien[7], in 2010 (II-17). The garden is enclosed by a crown of low artificial tree-covered elevations, and has in its southern part a winding lake, while a big hill marks the northern part. It thus reflects the principles of perimeter walls, northward protection and the presence of a pool of water; moreover it features a stream flowing through it out to the south. And it goes without saying that the entry to the botanical garden is on the southern side.

II-15 ——————————————————————————————— II-16 ———————————————

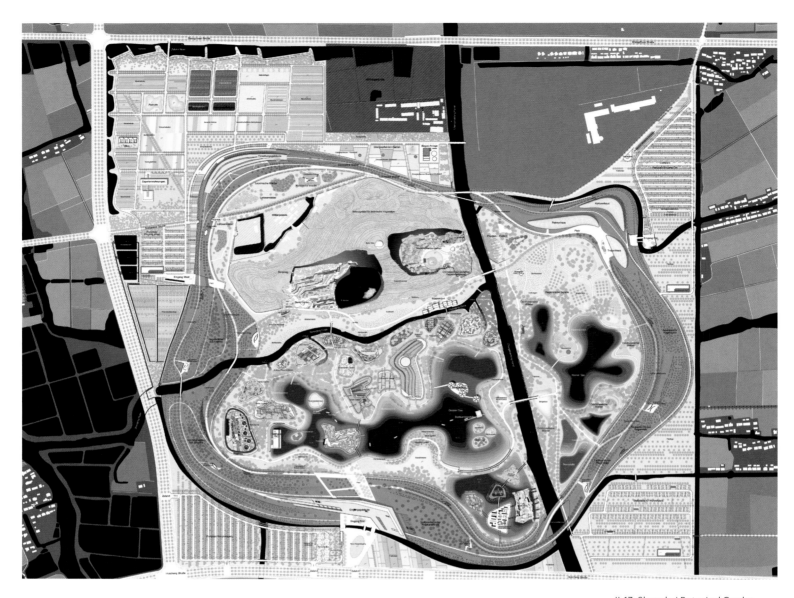

II-17: Shanghai Botanical Garden, Chenshan, Masterplan. The complex, built 2005-2010, is enclosed by a ring of elevations.

II-18: Shen Zhou (1427-1509), *Traveling in Xishan Mountains*. Handscroll, Ming dinasty.

II-17
II-18

Painting and Poetry

While adherence to the principles of *fengshui* guides the general distribution of the primary elements of the Chinese Garden, its narrative quality as visual account construed by a sequence of views of beautiful scenery is equally influenced by painting and poetry, in a sort of symbiotic development. The convergence is due to the fact that the Chinese meritocracy, through which the high state officials were chosen according to Confucian principles, required that its members study painting, poetry and calligraphy. These arts combined to affect the characteristics of gardens, whose owners for the most part belonged to a class of scholar-officials, the versatile aristocracy of state.

By the late Tang dynasty, in the mid-9th century, a period of political turmoil for China, the stylistic principles of landscape painting had found authoritative expression, and landscape painting emerged as an independent genre. It epitomized the longing of cultivated men to escape their quotidian world to feel in close spiritual contact with nature. As the Tang dynasty collapsed, the concept of withdrawal into the natural world became a major thematic focus of arts: faced with the failure of the human order, learned men sought permanence within the natural world. Painters represented dramatic aspects of the Chinese landscape, mountains and hills, deep gorges, mist-filled valleys, rivers and waterfalls – secluded places in which retreating from the chaos of dynastic disintegration and of the period of disunion which followed[8].

The works were composed on paper that was strong and at the same time flexible, so that it could be pasted onto canvas and form long rolls, which could be organized vertically and hung on walls, or horizontally, to form handscrolls. These could be several meters long, integrating true painting cycles or representing a whole natural microcosm. Scrolls of this kind are mounted on a roll and are opened from right to left, flat on a table, the viewer seeing no more than a segment at a time. The form of the horizontal scroll is a genuine visual device, bringing the observer to progress through a composition of many scenes following one another in linear succession, with multiple vanishing points, one fading imperceptibly into the next. As the landscape scroll is unrolled, the observer becomes part of it, entering into the artist's world of winding mountain paths, peaks and streams (II-18). This early technique reverberates in video animations visualizing contemporary projects for instance by Turenscape, where the common video strategy of "flying" over the terrain gains in cultural depth on the background of the traditional, horizontally manipulated handscroll[9].

The same spirit of progression through a multiple-faced landscape inspires the Chinese Garden. As the handscrolls are never spread out and viewed in their entirety, the green architectures are planned so as to never be perceived as a whole. Unrolling a scroll means following a story; by analogy, a person who experiences a garden enjoys a sequence of scenes which similarly make up a spatial narration, as they are related to each other.

Also the tradition of giving poetical names to some elements, a pavilion or sections of the garden, enhances the perception of the garden as a planned sequence of views (II-19; II-20). Names or quotations of literary passages offer an interpretation of the green space, revealing the owner's intentions in a play of cultured citations between man-made landscape and literary tradition[10]. The intellectual charge of the names and quotations associated with the various parts of the garden assumed an ever more important role, to the degree that they became a real challenge to owners of gardens. As a scholar of the Ming period, Chen Jiru (1550-1639), noted: "There are four difficulties with gardens: it is difficult to have fine mountains and waters; it is difficult to have old trees; it is difficult to plan; and it is difficult to assign names"[11].

II-19: Yu yuan, "Garden to Please", Shanghai. The inscription on the horizontal board introduces the scene behind the wall. It is composed of the character *liu*, flow, and the character *cui*, green. A possible transliteration reads "Flowing green". Both *liu* and *cui* conjure up the images of femininity in nature, suggesting that green water is flowing and moving like a woman.

II-20: Wangshi yuan, "Garden of the Master of the Fishing Nets", Suzhou. The inscription on the horizontal board is composed by the character *yun*, cloud, and the character *ku*, cave, cellar. The poetic implication of *ku* refers to a hideout. A possible transliteration, and the name of the scene behind the door, could read "Hideout in the clouds".

II-21; 22: Zhuozheng yuan, "Garden of the Humble Administrator", Suzhou. A covered walkway along a pond. The set itinerary of paths defines the rhythm of the garden's unfoldment.

The Spatial Framework

In his volume *On Chinese Gardens* published in 1984, the Chinese garden scholar Chen Congzhou (1918-2000) classified gardens in two categories: those intended for in-position viewing and those intended for in-motion viewing[12]. The first category, which concerns small gardens, links the appreciation of them to a stationary view gained by stopping movement, and this requires specific vantage points – a pavilion, a terrace – from which it is possible to view the green space. In the more extensive gardens or parks of the second type, visitors are led along a promenade which enables them to appreciate the great variety in composition. This subdivision of gardens into two classes is flexible, however, and often the two intentions overlap in the same garden; but Chen Congzhou's approach still has the merit of clarifying the link between motion, rest and the experience of gardens. The object of the composition of a Chinese Garden is the modulation of perception in a visual narration presupposing movement through its different parts at different paces, required or suggested by the formation of the spaces.

Let us consider the means used to shape the garden so that it can tell its story. The organizational pattern of spatial articulation in a Chinese Garden is hidden from the visitor and consists of a hierarchy of places and points. Each garden contains a certain number of spaces, each endowed with a specific characterization. We can call these thematic units. All units have a varying number of scenic views, each of which in turn concerns a portion of the unit's area and is made up of a defined viewing zone and of the *jing*, the view enjoyed[13]. The garden unfolds according to a predetermined itinerary for visitors, one that leads them through the individual thematic units and induces them to pause at the various viewing zones to enjoy the designed views. The paths thus define the sequence of the narration, the story line as it were, whose rhythm is set by the alternation of movement toward new spaces and pauses for admiration of the scenes (II-21).

The main walkway may offer alternative routes, temporarily running alongside or intersecting the main path. But all walkways have analogous characteristics: they all twist continually, with variations in gradient and paving, which, along with the succession of spaces and views, contribute to the sense of surprise and discovery (II-22).

The apparently casual winding of paths serves to multiply the viewing zones, offering a non-linear progression from one thematic unit to the next, from scenic view to scenic view, helping immerse the visitor in a kaleidoscope of situations. The process is enhanced by the strategy of mixing concealment and revelation along the path: sections of the garden first are occluded, then suggested through glimpses, and then progressively revealed according to the precise visual means selected for the appreciation of the respective portion of the garden (II-23).

The organization into thematic units and scenic views produces the typical Chinese Garden plan in its succession and in its different landscapes, adjacent to but hidden from one another. What reveals them to the visitor are the paths which serve as active agents of the garden, organizing movement through it, establishing places to pause, to slow down or speed up, thus defining the rhythm of the garden's unfolding (II-24).

II-23: Zhuozheng yuan, "Garden of the Humble Administrator", Suzhou. With its changes in gradients, the winding covered walkway contributes to the studied mix of concealment and revelation of sections of the garden along the paths.

II-24: Yu yuan, "Garden to Please", Shanghai. Openings along the wall dividing a double corridor offer glimpses on secluded parts of the garden.

II-25: Wangshi yuan, "Garden of the Master of the Fishing Nets", Suzhou. Delimited by walls, this courtyard constitutes a thematic unit within a defined perimeter.

II-26: Yu yuan. The pool with rocky shores planted with trees is an example of a thematic unit within a permeable perimeter.

II-27: Canglang ting, "Surging Waves Pavilion", Suzhou. A hill placed just behind the main entrance hides the view of the garden, increasing the sense of expectation.

II-23 ——————————————————————— II-24 ———————————

A Garden of Episodes

The general articulation of the garden is thus based on dividing its space into separate episodes or thematic units, which are the basic components of the garden's design.

These spaces are visually circumscribed and relatively autonomous, and each is characterized by its own aesthetic and formal identity. The thematic units are sometimes configured like proper rooms, as is the case of the courtyards delimited by walls (II-25). At other times the units take the form of less definite spaces, with permeable and porous perimeters, as is generally the case of reflecting pools and big rock formations (II-26). They can be adjacent to one another and even overlap, as happens in smaller gardens, or they can have filter zones, which in the case of imperial gardens can be quite extensive. Filter zones are also sometimes placed to mediate the units' relation with the different residential areas or with the external perimeter of the property. For the most part they constitute a connective tissue in which the thematic units float.

The subdivision of the garden's surface into thematic units creates a sort of visual tension for the visitor, along with a sense of expectation, heightened by the ways in which the various units are revealed one by one. The Chinese literary masterpiece, *Hong Lou Meng, The Dream of the Red Chamber*, written in the mid-18th century and attributed to Cao Xueqin, contains an account of a visit of a group of friends to the *Daguan yuan*, "Grand View Garden", a phantastic garden in which the drama is set. In crossing the green space, the group comes into disparate spaces hidden from one another, in line with a philosophy invoked in the first lines of the description: "When he [Chia Cheng] forthwith asked that the gate [of the garden] should be thrown open, all that met their eyes was a long stretch of verdant hills, which shut in the view in front of them. - What a fine hill, what a pretty hill! - exclaimed all the companions with one voice. - Were it not for this one hill - Chia Cheng explained - whatever scenery is contained in it would clearly strike the eye, as soon as one entered into the garden, and what pleasure would that have been?"[14] (II-27).

Perhaps it was traditional handscroll painting, which recounted stories and places in different episodes on a single scroll, that engendered this way of articulating gardens. Or perhaps, more simply, the narrative construction of a Chinese Garden is analogous with that of the scrolls.

The pictorial principle of separation of episodes has a counterpart in the garden's organization of the successive thematic units. If in a scroll painting the scenes are separated through a void of space, in the form of a depiction of a foggy zone or a riverbed or hill, in the garden the diverse thematic units are separated – and at the same time connected – by filter zones made of walls or rocky areas, covered walkways or wooded groves[15] (II-28). This idea of separation can already be perceived in the entrance to the garden, which is often narrow, never direct or particularly convenient. By creating physical and visual separation between the thematic units, these elements constitute larger or smaller moments of suspension and pause, as a prelude to the next thematic unit (II-29; II-30).

The succession of thematic units and the ensuing juxtaposition of different ambiances lend the garden a kind of geographic dimension: in the garden described in *The Dream of the Red Chamber*, a verdant hill is followed by a cave, a winding stream, a pond, an orchard, a paddy and enclosed green courtyards. Passing from a literary garden to a real one, the composition is equally varied. In the *Wangshi yuan*, "Garden of the Master of the Fishing Nets", in the city of Suzhou, originally created in the early 12th century to be completely redesigned in the second half of the 18th century (II-31), the variety of thematic units includes a rock garden featuring a precious pavilion, a lake where small buildings simulate a village, a paved court with big rocks and a spring, a sequence of smaller courts with rock compositions and a flower garden (II-32). The *Yu yuan*, "Garden to Please", in Shanghai (II-33) features a mountain next to a pond, a rushing stream, hillside pavilions, a big lake crossed by bridges, a reflecting pool with a vertical rock composition, a sequence of paved courts and a rock labyrinth with little studios (II-34). The garden was originally created between 1559 and 1577 and much altered over the years.

II-28: Yi yuan, "Joyful Garden", Suzhou. The double covered walkway separates two contiguous thematic units.

II-29: Yu yuan, "Garden to Please", Shanghai. A wall acts as separation between two sequential thematic units.

II-30: Yu yuan. Two thematic units are divided by a white wall and connected by a passageway through a rocky composition.

II-31: Wangshi yuan, "Garden of the Master of the Fishing Nets", Suzhou. Plan of the current layout of the garden.

II-32: Wangshi yuan. Plan showing the thematic units according to which the garden is subdivided.

Composition and Effects

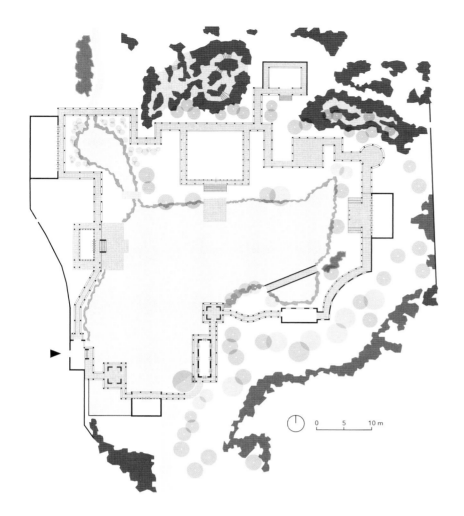

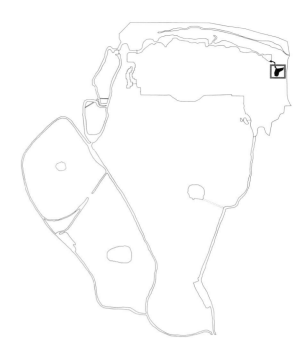

II-35: Xiequ yuan, "Garden of Harmonious Interest", within the Yihe yuan, Beijing. The garden is arranged around a lake, which is surrounded by a ring of covered walkways and a garland of pavilions.

II-36: Xiequ yuan. Plan of the current layout of the garden (left) and scheme of its location within the Yihe yuan imperial park (right).

II-36

Scenic Views

The sequence of thematic units ensures dynamic enjoyment of the garden. The other aspect of its perception comes, by contrast, from pauses and relates to scenic views. These are static pictures conceived to attract the eye and awaken different sensations: elegance, majesty, astonishment.

Each thematic unit, according to its extension and configuration, may be linked to a single scenic view or offer many of them. The scenic views are enjoyed for their aesthetic and compositional quality, and are made up of two distinct but associated parts: the picture offered for view and the area prepared for admiration of the view.

Elements of formal identity characterize the scenic views, giving each its own compositional harmony. The character of a specific scene can originate in a complex composition: a lake with buildings reflected in it or a waterfall coming down from a group of rocks. But it can also be given by simple elements: a sculptural rock in a bamboo grove, a pavilion shaded by willows. Or a seasonal characterization may prevail, generated by particular flowers or leaf colors. For example, the *Ge yuan*, "Isolated Garden", in Yangzhou, probably created in the second half of the 17th century and remodeled in the 19th century, presents four distinct scenic views which evoke the seasons: they are characterized by four different rocky compositions, built of different types of stone and surrounded by different plants (II-37).

Because they are static pictures, the scenes are abstract and meditative; they imply the visitor's participation in interpreting them and his willingness to be transported into an immaterial place through the visual experience of the physical environment.

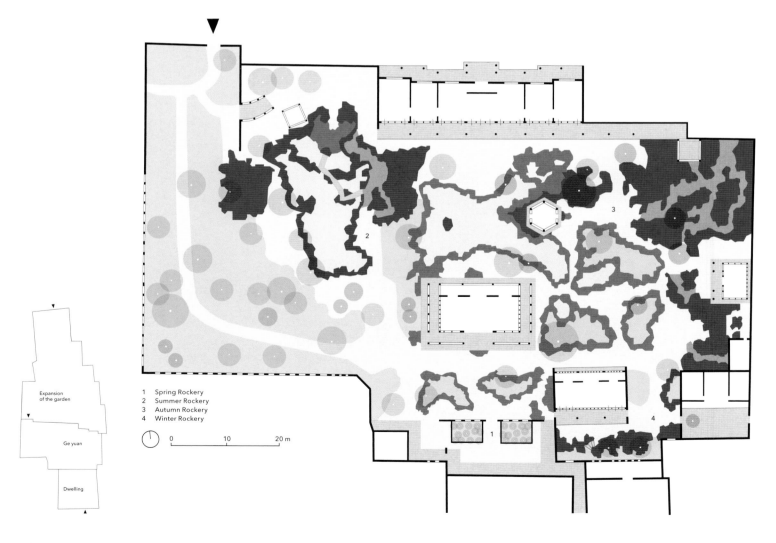

Expansion
of the garden

Ge yuan

Dwelling

1 Spring Rockery
2 Summer Rockery
3 Autumn Rockery
4 Winter Rockery

0   10   20 m

A series of devices favor this form of intellectual enjoyment: some scenic views refer to well-known paintings or landscapes, or include literary references, or bear poetical names. A visit to any garden entails reading inscriptions and name plaques in the elegant Chinese self-expressive calligraphy on stone, wood or paper, placed on walls and pavilions. The inscriptions carry the names the owner has given to parts of the garden, a scene, a view, a pavilion, or they are verses or literary passages evoked by the part of the garden that is being discovered. In the *Liu yuan*, "Lingering Garden", in Suzhou, which dates back to the first half of the 16th century and was rebuilt in the early 19th century, the pavilions composing a series of scenic views beyond the central reflecting pool have names referring to verses of famous Chinese poets: Passable Pavilion, Refreshing Breeze Pavilion, Winding Stream Tower, Green Shade Pavilion (II-38), while a small pond featuring an imposing sculptural rock in the northeastern part of the garden is called Washing Clouds Pool (II-39). These appealing features engender emotional responses in the observer and form the evocative counterpart of the scenery, loading it with deeper meanings and symbols, suggesting poetic allusions and arousing sentiments: appreciation of gardens involves imaginative engagement.

In addition to poetical references, scenic views succeed by enhancing visual perception: first of all depth of field and framing.

The Chinese Garden alternates scenic views with different depths of field, thus keeping perception ever keen. Scenes with a short depth of field emphasize the subject close to the observer; this is the case of the stunning rocks exhibited in courtyards, or of the collections of potted landscapes that need to be appreciated from up close (II-40). In this case, the background limiting the view, usually a wall, is given a neutral treatment so as to offset the principle subject of the scene.

II-37: Ge yuan, "Isolated Garden", Yangzhou. Plan of the garden.

II-38: Liu yuan, "Lingering Garden", Suzhou. The Winding Stream Tower and the Green Shade Pavilion are elements of the scenic views composed around the lake.

II-39: Liu yuan. The little pond dominated by a tall rock is the highlight of a paved courtyard with rockeries and pavilions.

II-40: Shizi lin, "Lion Grove", Suzhou. An example of a scene with a short depth of field: sculptural rocks exhibited at the center of a paved courtyard.

II-38

II-39

II-40

63

When the scene calls for a medium or long depth of field, the composition takes advantage of the positioning of various elements at increasing distances from the observer (II-41). This is the "principle of the three depths", a pictorial convention of Chinese landscape painting[16]. It consists in configuring the foreground, the middle ground and the background of each single scene according to a sequence of planes (II-42; II-43; II-44), increasing the sense of depth and thereby influencing the perception of the scale of the whole.

The construction of a scene with a long depth of field can adopt the compositional technique called *jiejing*, "borrowed scenery"[17]. This entails bringing into the scenic view what lies beyond the garden walls, framing portions of the outside landscape near and far, as a chain of hills or a high pagoda (II-45). That establishes a relation between what is near and what is far, merging the sweep of the view into the larger landscape, which functions as a background for the garden's design. The garden, thus linked with the landscape beyond, seems in this way to become boundless (II-46). Some gardens in areas enjoying unique natural landscapes feature pavilions or belvedere terraces as viewpoints from which to enjoy the panorama beyond the garden. In the *Ou yuan*, "Couple's Garden Retreat", in Suzhou a two-storied edifice built along the eastern boundary of the garden offers a view onto the canal that runs alongside the green space (II-47).

The perception of the borrowed scenery represents a moment of interruption of the enclosure inside which the garden composition unwinds. While the Chinese Garden presents a continuously introverted mechanism of spatial arrangement and scenic organization, the borrowed scenery creates an instant of exceptionality, breaking the perimeter wall by using a feature which physically does not belong to the context of the garden. From this point of view, it is rather different from the technique of the borrowed landscape which establishes a spatial continuity between garden and landscape in the English Landscape Garden, because the latter is instead based on the visual – and, at the same time, ideological – negation of the boundaries of the park.

II-41: Liu yuan, "Lingering Garden", Suzhou. A view from a pavilion overlooking the water provides an example for a scene characterized by a medium depth of field.

II-42: Wangshi yuan, "Garden of the Master of the Fishing Nets", Suzhou. The group of pavilions arranged on the shore of a lake, as viewed from the opposing pavilion, is an example of a scene with a long depth of field.

II-43: Shanghai Houtan Park, Shanghai. The steel-colored structure of a former industrial pavilion is the focus of a scene composed according to a sequence of planes.

II-44: Olympic Forest Park, Beijing. The pavilions along the shore of the lake form the center of the scene, as seen from the opposing elevation.

II-45; 46: Yihe yuan, "Garden of the Preservation of Harmony", Beijing. The imperial garden integrates the landscape scenery of the West Hills beyond its walls as part of a total composition achieved through the technique of the *jiejing*, "borrowed scenery".

II-47: Ou yuan, "Couple's Garden Retreat", Suzhou. Emerging from the continuous enclosing wall, a two-storied pavilion offers views onto the canals surrounding the garden.

1: Attiret, "Lettre", 7. Translation by the author.

2: On *fengshui*, see for example Joseph Needham, *Science and Civilization in China: Volume II, History of Scientific Thought* (Cambridge: Cambridge University Press, 1991), 359-63; Yves Kirchner, "Rituals and traditions of Chinese space", in *In the Chinese city. Perspectives on the transmutation of an empire*, ed. Frédéric Edelmann (Barcelona: Actar, 2008), 160-67.

3: In geomancy, the four cardinal directions are associated with animals, real or mythical: the Red Bird equated the southern quarter, the Blue Dragon the eastern quarter, the Black Turtle the northern quarter and the White Tiger was associated to the western quarter.

4: As Hui Zhou recalls, "Although the role of *fengshui* was crucial in garden planning and especially so for imperial gardens, it was never elevated to the level of garden theory that was highly developed in private gardens". See Zhou, "The *jing*", 326, note 21. In fact, in the *Yuanye*, a treatise written in the first half of the 17th century on the principles and techniques of planning, *fengshui* is never mentioned. On the role of *fengshui* in Chinese Garden design, see also Wong Yong-tsu, *A Paradise Lost. The Imperial Garden of Yuanming Yuan* (Honululu, HI: University of Hawaii Press, 2001), 21-22.

5: Jingshan Mountain is 40 m high; Yangshan Mountain, in Olympic Forest Park, rises 48 m. It was created with the earth dug out for the new section of the subway system that leads to the park, as well as for the construction of Olympic Avenue and other nearby urban development. Liu Hui and Zhao Jing, eds., *Olympic Forest Park Planning and Design* (Beijing: Beijing Tsinghua Urban Planning and Design Institute, 2008), 14-15.

6: Zhou, "The *jing*", 296.

7: The project was in collaboration with Straub+Thurmayr Landschaftsarchitekten and Auer+Weber+Assoziierte Architekten.

8: In this period, known as the Five Dynasties (907-960), northern China was ruled by five short-lived military regimes. See Keay, *China*, 290-300.

9: See the examples of presentation videos on the Shanghai Green Dragon Park and the Changsha Oranges Island project by Turenscape on the DVD included in the book by Elke Mertens, *Visualizing Landscape Architecture* (Basel, Boston, Berlin: Birkhäuser, 2009).

10: For an analysis of the role and meaning of names in the Chinese Garden, see John Makeham, "The Confucian Role of Names in Traditional Chinese Gardens", *Studies in the History of Gardens & Designed Landscapes* 18, 3 (1998): 192-95.

11: Quoted in *Ibid.*, 193.

12: Chen Congzhou, *On Chinese Gardens*, trans. Chen Xiongshan et al. (Shanghai: Shanghai Press, 2009), 15. Chen's five essays in *On Chinese Gardens* were written between 1978 and 1982. They were first printed in the Journal of the Tongji University in separate issues. In 1984 they were published in a bilingual edition - Chinese and English - by the Tongji University Press.

13: The layout of Chinese Gardens as an itinerary through different connected scenes to be observed from specific points was perceived in the mid-18th century by the Swedish-born architect William Chambers. In his book *Design of Chinese Buildings, Furniture, Dresses, Machines, and Utensils*, published in London in 1757, he explains that "the whole ground [of the garden] is laid out in a variety of scenes, and you are led, by winding passages cut in the groves, to the different points of view, each of which is marked by a seat, a building, or some other objects. The perfection of their gardens consists in the number, beauty, and diversity of these scenes". Quoted in John Dixon Hunt and Peter Willis, eds., *The Genius of the Place. The English Landscape Garden 1620-1820* (Cambridge, MA: The MIT Press, 1998²).

14: Cao Xueqin, *The Dream of the Red Chamber*, transl. H. Bencraft Joly, web edition published by the University of Adelaide, eBooks@Adelaide, 2009, chapter 17. http://ebooks.adelaide.edu.au/c/cao_xueqin/c2359h/complete.html

15: On the concept of separation in the Chinese Garden see: Chung Wah Nan, "La création contemporaine: l'héritage du ting", in Baud-Berthier, Couëtoux, Chiu, *Le Jardin*, 211-12. See also Frances Ya-Sing Tsu, *Landscape design in Chinese gardens* (New York: McGraw-Hill, 1988), 136.

16: George Rowley notes: "The Chinese perfected the principle of the three depths, according to which spatial depth was marked by a foreground, middle distance, and far distance, each parallel to the picture plane, so that the eye leapt from one distance to the next through a void of space". See George Rowley, *Principles of Chinese Painting* (Princeton, NJ: Princeton University Press, 1974), 64.

17: For the compositional technique of borrowed scenery, see Ji Cheng, *The Craft of Gardens - Yuan ye*, trans. Alison Hardie (New Haven, CT: Yale University Press, 1988), 119-21. See also Che Bing Chiu, "The traditional Chinese Garden: a world apart", in *In the Chinese city*, ed. Edelmann, 64-65. The principle of "borrowed scenery", by which a distant view is incorporated into the garden, enjoyed a great fortune in Japan as well, where it took the name *shakkei*. It was often applied in creating stroll gardens; the imperial villa Shigaku-in in Kyoto is one of the most interesting uses of the technique. See Marc Treib, "Moving the Eye", in *Sites Unseen. Landscape and Vision*, ed. Diane Harris and D. Fairchild Ruggles (Pittsburgh, PA: University of Pittsburgh Press, 2007), 86.

18: For an extensive analysis of the role of door and window openings in Chinese Gardens see Antoine Gournay, "Le système des ouvertures dans l'aménagement spatial du jardin chinois", *Extrême-Orient, Extrême-Occident* 22: *L'art des jardins dans les pays sinisés* (2000): 51-71.

Chapter 3

Elements

According to ancient animistic beliefs, rocks were the earth's skeleton and rivers its arteries, living elements that were complementary in the harmony of the cosmos. Water and mountains represented the fertile juxtaposition between *yin* and *yang*, the dualism of the feminine and masculine aspects present in all natural phenomena. The robust vigor of rocks evinced the solid masculine element, while water's fluidity suggested the changeable feminine.

Thus every garden needs to evoke the mountains and bodies of water, even if only in metaphorical miniaturized form. The marriage of these two elements constitutes the primary goal of the creative effort (III-2). To these primary elements are added flora, whose changes introduce the dimension of seasonal cycles and thereby time into the garden, and architecture. The pavilions dotting the garden denote the human presence in nature and the central role of the individual in the imaginative and poetical interpretation of the landscape.

III-1: Hengshan Hanging Temple, Hengshan. The monastery complex consists of wooden pavilions connected by walkways built on the cliff face of a sacred Daoist mountain.

III-2: Yi yuan, "Joyful Garden", Suzhou. Chinese Gardens feature one or several ponds and rock compositions. The fluidity of water corresponds with the solidity of the rocks, while also acting as a reflecting surface.

III-3: Yihe yuan, "Garden of the Preservation of Harmony", Beijing. A group of buildings arranged on the rocky hillside south of Longevity Hill.

III-4: Shizi lin, "Lion Grove", Suzhou. A sculptural rock rising from the waters of the lake.

III-5: Liu yuan, "Lingering Garden", Suzhou. Its preeminent position within an open courtyard exalts the formal qualities of the vertical rock.

III-6: Canglang ting, "Surging Waves Pavilion", Suzhou. A single rock of bizarre form is placed at the top of an artificial mountain.

III-7: Shizi lin. The garden features many sculptural rocks, whose characteristics evoke the aspect of a lion.

III-1 ——————————————————————————————— III-2 ———————————————

III-3 ———————————————

Mounds and Rocky Compositions

The sacred nature of mountains in China has been evidenced by a preference for mountain sites for the construction of temples and monasteries, sometimes even in places that appear wholly hostile to human life, thereby displaying the will to commune uncompromisingly with the natural environment (III-1). In gardens, mountains are represented by the use of rocks. Through time a strong aesthetic sensitivity for rocks developed, and led to widespread collecting of them (III-3).

Rocks are placed in many different settings in gardens, but they are used in two main ways: single rocks as sculptures and rock compositions as artificial mountains[1].

Sculptural rocks are individual stones of particular elegance, or simple compositions of such stones that can be placed so as to exalt the formal quality of each single piece (III-4; III-5). Rocks are also considered in relation to each other; delicate stones suggesting feminine qualities are balanced with rugged ones considered to represent the masculine. Single stone blocks are chosen for their characteristic qualities: conformation, substance, color, texture, presence of fissures and openings, veins. In the search for and choice of rocks, preference is given to those with animal and human shapes, or those displaying signs of erosion by water and wind, thus evoking the passage of time, or again those whose particular characteristics might serve to invoke landscapes presented in literature or in paintings (III-6; III-7). The best stones for these characteristics are sedimentary rocks quarried in mountains or taken from lakes and rivers. Northern China is rich in calcites, but it is the region near the Yangtze River delta, in the central-eastern part of the country, that is best known for its abundance and diversity of rocks[2].

III-4

III-5

III-6

III-7

The rocks are either placed directly on the ground, or arranged on a base. The bases are sometimes decorated, presenting the stone similar to a sculpture.

Rocks can be gathered together to form little collections or rock gardens. Often they are displayed at a central point within a small courtyard, or they are positioned against a wall, which eliminates visual interference and permits full appreciation of their beauty (III-9). Positioned near the main pavilions or covered walkways, their proximity to architectural elements creates an effective contrast between nature and architecture (III-10). And they can be associated with exceptional plant specimens, like an old pine or a tree with extraordinary branches; bushes or flowers can be planted in the cavities of rough stones, thus creating a natural micro-landscape.

Artificial mountains, on the other hand, are compact structures formed by rocks and earth, or by large rocks assembled and held together with mortar (III-11). Their forms evoke varying natural types of morphology, and they are intended to awaken visitors' emotions. Mountains and cliffs suggest wild nature; meanders and grottos astonish; rushing waters and cascades recall the flow of life. Because of this symbolic charge, mountains are never placed in the central space of the garden, but rather dispersed around the whole garden, so that their visual importance and the energy they possess do not dominate the whole composition (III-8).

The fabrication of artificial mountains is a weighty commitment, similar to constructing a building. Foundations capable of sustaining their weight have to be created, often by digging tree trunks into the ground to make a stable base. On this underpinning are placed solid monoliths, stones regular in shape with surfaces smooth enough to form a good basis. The upper part is made up of smaller rocks with less robust forms, put together in such a way as to give the mountain a mimetic, highly varied form.

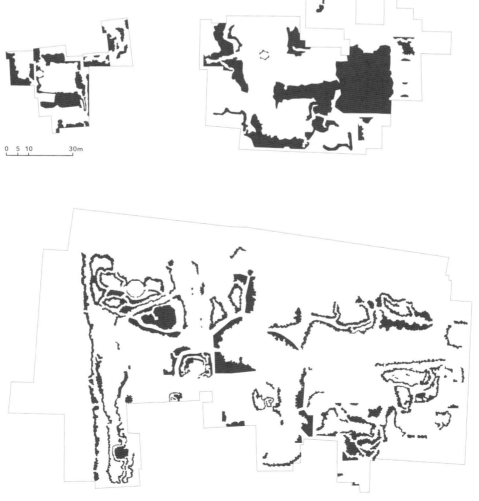

0 5 10   30m

III-8

III-8: Schemes of rockeries distribution in the gardens of Wangshi yuan, "Garden of the Master of the Fishing Nets", Shizi lin, "Lion Grove" and Zhuozheng yuan, "Garden of the Humble Administrator", in Suzhou.

III-9: Yu yuan, "Garden to Please", Shanghai. A linear artificial hill offset against a white wall.

III-10: Shizi lin, "Lion Grove", Suzhou. Hidden by a rocky mountain, the pavilion creates an effect of contrast between architecture and nature.

III-11: Yuhua yuan, "Back Garden of the Imperial Palace", Forbidden City, Beijing. The artificial mountain is topped with a pavilion-belvedere.

III-9

III-10

III-11

III-12: Yu yuan, "Garden to Please", Shanghai. Piles of stones rise from the rocky shore of a stream.

III-13: Shizi lin, "Lion Grove", Suzhou. Overlooking the lake, an artificial mountain chain forms a complex structure with caves, defiles and isolated peaks made of single rocks.

III-14: Yu yuan. A rocky shore introduces a rugged separation between the flat plains of water and pathway.

III-15: Shizi lin. The garden composition plays on the ingenious and pervasive use of rocks.

The artificial mountains' summits are made up of single rocks forming isolated peaks or crests. There can be multiple peaks without apparent order, or a main summit can be surrounded by secondary ones. Fantasy mountain chains can thus be created, while others are reminiscent of specific existing heights or rock formations (III-12). The stone compositions can feature defiles or meanders or caves leading the visitor into the mountain itself or even up toward the summit. Terraces and belvederes with picturesque pavilions along the way offer privileged views of the surroundings. In order to accentuate the verisimilitude of the mountain scene, pines and other trees are planted among the rocks, correlated in height with the artificial mountain and controlled in growth so as to maintain their reciprocal scale. In addition to serving as sculptures and artificial mountains, rocks are also adopted to create the shores of ponds and streams, while flat rocks are placed on the stream beds to create fords for crossing (III-13).

Gardens that present today impressive and beautiful rock compositions include the *Shizi lin* in the city of Suzhou, and the *Yu yuan* in Shanghai. In the *Shizi lin*, "Lion Grove", the visitor arrives through a sequence of regular courts displaying arrangements of sculptural rocks, leading into an area where great rocks atop one another are reminiscent of a mountain chain, with narrow defiles and grottos, while the path becomes a series of rapid ascents and descents. The artificial mountain conceals a large artificial lake encircled by jagged boulders, on which single vertical stones were placed to suggest the body or head of lions in various positions (III-14). In Shanghai's *Yu yuan*, "Garden to Please", rocks again dominate the composition. The garden combines a yellow granite mountain, a long rockery set against a wall, a sequence of high rockworks on which various pavilions are built, and stony passageways. Different types of rocks are bordering the ponds within the garden. A composition of three sculptural rocks evoking a mountainous landscape overlooks a pool (III-15). The symbolic and compositional value of rocks emerges in some contemporary landscape architecture projects in China as well. The Olympic Forest Park of Beijing includes some

big rock compositions near pine groves, a feature traditional in taste (III-16); there is also a great streaked stone mass which greets visitors at the entrance (III-17). A heterodox and more poetical use of rock is that of the architect and artist Ai Weiwei in his project for the banks of the Yiwu River, which crosses the city of Jinhua, south of Shanghai. Completed in 2004, the project entailed building wide promenades on both sides of the river (III-18). Using local granite, Ai Weiwei has transformed the riverbanks into a tectonic structure terraced down toward the water. The forms are sharp and highly sculptural, evoking rocky bluffs in a dialogue with the distant mountain chain that closes the horizon (III-19).

III-16: Olympic Forest Park, Beijing. The highest point in the park features a composition of massive rocks set among pines.

III-17: Olympic Forest Park. The great single stone placed at the entrance of the park.

III-18: Yiwu Riverbank, Jinhua. Built in 2002-2004, the new riverbanks, made of local granite, feature walkways, steps and platforms harmonized with sculptural forms.

III-19: Yiwu Riverbank. The sharp edges of the banks, which originated from a flood control project, establish a poetic dialogue with the distant mountains.

III-20: Liu yuan, "Lingering Garden", Suzhou. The garden is centered on an irregularly-shaped lake dominated by an artificial mountain with a belvedere.

III-21: Schemes of water distribution in the gardens of Wangshi yuan, "Garden of the Master of the Fishing Nets", Shizi lin, "Lion Grove" and Zhuozheng yuan, "Garden of the Humble Administrator", in Suzhou.

III-16 ——————————————————————————————————

III-18 ——————————————————————————————————

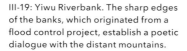

III-17 ——————————————————————————————————

III-19 ——————————————————————————————————

Water Surfaces

Historically, the Chinese countryside's most evolved areas were characterized by rice paddies. The flooding of these fields was regulated by complex hydraulic systems which provided the water necessary for a crop on which the prosperity of entire regions depended. With their shining surfaces animated by birds and the brilliant green of their vegetation, with their adherence to the terrain's morphology and their areas interspersed with little groves of trees or bamboo, traditional rice paddies are among the most pleasing landscapes ever created by man. It is not unlikely that they became one of the original inspirations for Chinese Gardens.

Surface water's liquid horizontality, contrasted with the stony verticality of rocks, makes it the second foundational element of the Chinese Garden (III-20). The presence of water conveys a sense of spaciousness, dynamism and vitality to the composition; by adding the dimension of sound – the gurgling of streams and the splashing of carps – it responds to the principles of *fengshui*, according to which reflecting pools are reservoirs of positive energies. They also improve the local microclimate. For all these reasons, when water was available it was allocated significant space: in the city of Suzhou, which is crossed by canals, waters cover on the average half of the gardens' surfaces; in Beijing, three quarters of the *Yihe yuan* park is covered by water (III-21). The pervasive presence of water in various forms is the distinguishing trait of some gardens. Such is the case of the *Zhuozheng yuan*, "Garden of the Humble Administrator", in Suzhou, an artificial lagoon on an extensive urban property, marked by a series of irregularly shaped islets adorned with the garden's various pavilions (III-22). The current design of the garden features a succession of peninsulas and isles linked by zigzagging bridges, with tongues of water between rocks and pavilions (III-23; III-24).

0 5 10   30 m

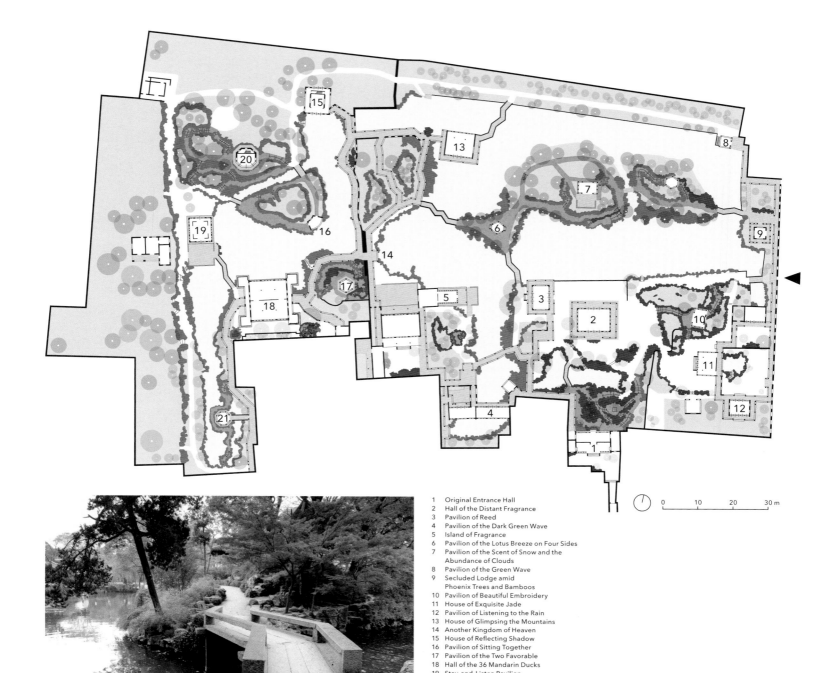

1 Original Entrance Hall
2 Hall of the Distant Fragrance
3 Pavilion of Reed
4 Pavilion of the Dark Green Wave
5 Island of Fragrance
6 Pavilion of the Lotus Breeze on Four Sides
7 Pavilion of the Scent of Snow and the
   Abundance of Clouds
8 Pavilion of the Green Wave
9 Secluded Lodge amid
   Phoenix Trees and Bamboos
10 Pavilion of Beautiful Embroidery
11 House of Exquisite Jade
12 Pavilion of Listening to the Rain
13 House of Glimpsing the Mountains
14 Another Kingdom of Heaven
15 House of Reflecting Shadow
16 Pavilion of Sitting Together
17 Pavilion of the Two Favorable
18 Hall of the 36 Mandarin Ducks
19 Stay-and-Listen Pavilion
20 Pavilion of Floating Jade
21 Pavilion of the Reflected Pergola

III-22: Zhuozheng yuan, "Garden of the Humble Administrator", Suzhou. Plan of the garden.

III-23: Zhuozheng yuan. This large garden is designed as a series of connected pools with islands.

III-24: Zhuozheng yuan. Three ways of enjoying the water view: a covered walkway, an open-air path, a pavilion to sit.

III-25: Wangshi yuan, "Garden of the Master of the Fishing Nets", Suzhou. The pond is the central element around which interconnected courtyards and pavilions are arranged.

III-26: Liu yuan, "Lingering Garden", Suzhou. The height of the pavilions and the breadth of the lake match to ensure the reflection of the complete scene.

III-27: Chi Lin Nunnery, Hong Kong. A reflecting pool of regular shape is delimitated by marble edges topped with balustrades.

III-22 ——————————
III-23 ——————————————————————————— III-24 ——————

Water is used in a multitude of ways, evoking its many changing forms in nature; it is concentrated in ponds usually located at the heart of the garden, running out in brooks that then cross the different parts of the green space (III-25). In its wide range of apparitions, it adopts different intensities of movement: in fishponds and basins it is relatively still; it moves at different speeds in streams, torrents and waterfalls. In all cases, it is not the depth of the water which is important, but its surface appearance, shape and sinuosity. Its reflecting quality is highly sought after, and for this reason pavilions and rock compositions are often situated near still water surfaces. It is a common design intention that they should be mirrored in their entirety; therefore the proportional relations between the dimensions of reflecting pools and of the objects to be reflected are carefully studied (III-26).

Reflecting pools are generally delimited by sinuous rock borders, with inlets, promontories and belvederes jutting out over the water. But there are also basins of regular quadrangular shapes, whose geometry is underscored by marble steps and balustrades (III-27). If the reflecting pool is large enough, islands are created in it. They can be irregular in outline or perfectly circular, rather flat or displaying steep heights; they may also feature little groves of trees, simple pavilions or complex works of architecture.

In the larger dimensions of imperial parks, the waters of artificial lakes are sometimes subdivided into different sections by earthen dykes. This is the case of the Kunming Lake in the imperial park of *Yihe yuan*, where a long dyke planted with trees separates the main lake from an area with secondary bodies of water.

III-25

III-26

III-27

Streams never ran straight. They can appear as rustic creeks with overgrown banks, or rocky mountain torrents (III-30), or they can also take man-made forms like canals with artificial embankments; this is the case of the elegant stream curving across the Forbidden City, or the irregularly edged canal along Suzhou Street in *Yihe yuan*. A garden's waters are to appear to come from a natural spring, and therefore water is channeled to a high point from which the system is supplied. From there, a little waterfall spurts through the rocky wall of a mountain, or a brook rushes into the main reflecting pool.

The traditional Chinese Garden's use of islets and winding waterways was given a recent ecological updating in several projects by the landscape architect Kongjian Yu of Turenscape, like the restoration of the beach along the Bohai Sea in the city of Qinhuangdao, east of Beijing, completed in 2008 (III-29). This project's goal was to transform a section of coastal dunes and adjacent wetland that had been degraded by previous uses, which left the site in an ecologically and environmentally damaged condition. Environmental recovery included the creation of a group of round islets in an existing pool of water, both to make the landscape more interesting and to attract birds (III-28); concurrently, a counter-image of the lake with islets was created closer to the shore, where little round ponds were dug in the flat ground, recomposing the wetland (III-31).

III-28

III-28: Qinhuangdao Beach Restoration, Qinhuangdao. A group of round islets set into the existing lake. The park was constructed between 2006 and 2008.

III-29: Qinhuangdao Beach Restoration. Masterplan.

III-30: Yu yuan, "Garden to Please", Shanghai. A gorge bordered by high artificial rock compositions.

III-31: Qinhuangdao Beach Restoration. In the central part of the park little round ponds were dug to recompose the wetland.

III-30

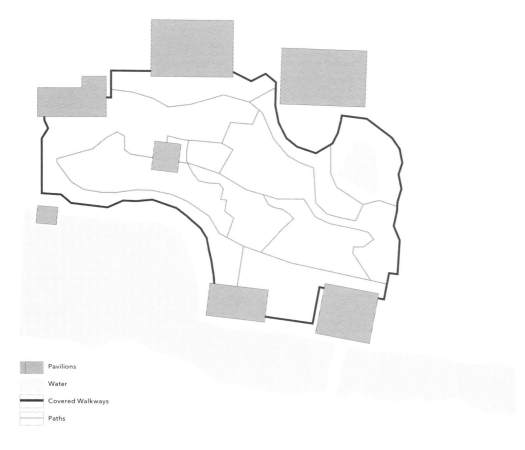

Pavilions

Water

Covered Walkways

Paths

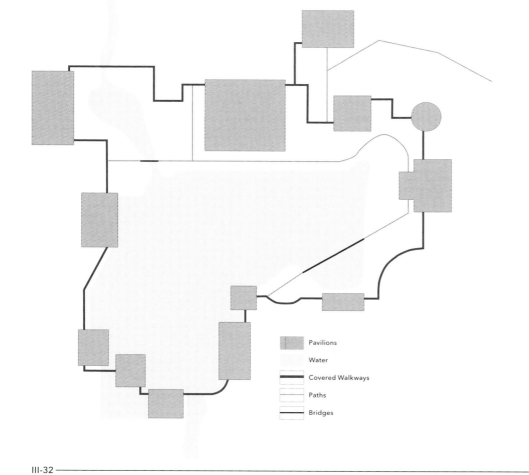

Pavilions

Water

Covered Walkways

Paths

Bridges

III-32 ——

III-33 ——

III-34 ————————————————————

III-35 ————————————————————

III-36 ————————————————————

Elements

Garden Paths

In creating a Chinese Garden, the designer aimes at laying out a pathway along which the various components of the green space would gradually reveal themselves to the visitor. It is this mechanism of a series of unexpected scenes that is to induce the visitor to investigate the entire garden (III-38).

The play of progressive disclosure depends on twisting and winding paths. Leading from a building to a grove, following the shore of a pond, insinuating themselves between rock formations, the walkways serve the function not only of linking all the various parts of the garden, but of determining the sequence or story-board of its narrative. The system of footpaths orients the movement of the visitor toward defined points, and changes in the track's paving material and elevation determine the tempi of perception of the scenes. The paths thus constitute a key element in the orchestration of the garden's story – but the composer behind it all has to remain hidden (III-32; III-33).

One characteristic is common to all paths: they are never linear except for short sections. Following the principles of *fengshui* and the inspiration of the natural environment, the paths can be twisting, zigzagging, or form a series of broken curves (III-34; III-35). Changes in height add to the intended unpredictability, contrived by adding ramps, steps and little bridges; changes in width likewise make for variety (III-37). The careful planning behind all this must never show, and the paths' variations are to seem simply an adaptation to the irregular topography of the site. Following this principle, narrow paths are also made meandering among compositions of rocks, just like in the garden described in the novel *The Dream of the Red Chamber* where the visitors encountered "white rugged rocks looking either like goblins, or resembling savage beasts, lying either crossways, or in horizontal or upright positions; on the surface of which grew moss and lichen with mottled hues, or parasitic plants, which screened off the light; while, slightly visible, wound, among the rocks, a narrow pathway like the intestines of a sheep"[3] (III-36).

III-32: Canglang ting, "Surging Waves Pavilion", Suzhou. Scheme of the garden paths.

III-33: Xiequ yuan, "Garden of Harmonious Interest", within the Yihe yuan, Beijing. Scheme of the garden paths.

III-34: Wangshi yuan, "Garden of the Master of the Fishing Nets", Suzhou. A zigzagging covered walkway.

III-35: Olympic Forest Park, Beijing. A sequence of large curves characterizes a main route within the park.

III-36: Yu yuan, "Garden to Please", Shanghai. A narrow path meandering among rocks.

III-37: Zhuozheng yuan, "Garden of the Humble Administrator", Suzhou. A long covered walkway built alongside a wall runs by the shore of a pool; the continuous variations in the inclination of

ramps produce changing perceptions of the reflecting flat water surface.

III-38: Xiaoying zhou, "Small Seas Islet", West Lake, Hangzhou. A winding bridge interconnecting water pavilions.

III-37 ——————————————————————————

III-38 ——

III-39: Xiequ yuan, "Garden of Harmonious Interest", within the Yihe yuan, Beijing. A winding covered walkway, open on either side, connects various pavilions.

III-40: Shizi lin, "Lion Grove", Suzhou. The route follows a sequence of contrasts: a stone bridge zigzagging over water, a meander inside a cave.

III-41: Wangshi yuan, "Garden of the Master of the Fishing Nets", Suzhou. The crooked shape of the stone bridge is accentuated by the slanting pine.

III-42: Yihe yuan, "Garden of the Preservation of Harmony", Beijing. A stone bridge supported by a semi-circular stone arch bridging a wide canal. The semi-circular form of the arch and its reflection generate a perfectly round shape.

III-43: Yu yuan, "Garden to Please", Shanghai. The winding footbridge seems to float over the waters of the lake.

III-44: Tianjin Waterfront Corridor, Tianjin. Twisting paths over shallow water allow a playful use of the space of the public park, designed 2005-2008.

III-39 ———————————— III-40 ————————————
III-41 ———————————— III-42 ————————————

In addition to open-air paths, there are covered walkways, which serve not only to protect visitors from the weather, but also to alter the luminosity and therefore the perception of the various parts of the garden. Their covering often consists of a tiled roof upheld by round or square slender columns of lacquered wood, interconnected by a low balustrade. The galleries thus formed may be open on either side to allow a wider view, or built alongside a wall which in turn can be solid but also punctured by screened openings, thereby allowing glimpses of the adjacent garden space (III-39). As an alternative, the covering of a path can consist of simple pergolas, overgrown by flowering plants like wisteria.

Brooks and inlets serve as occasions for constructing the many types of bridges the Chinese garden tradition is famous for; these can be rectilinear or zigzag, of wood or stone, supported by a single arch or a series of arches that are not necessarily symmetrical (III-40; III-41; III-42). Where the intention is to give the visitor a more direct contact with the water, the bridges become flat footbridges made of planks or paving stones, without parapets and so close to the water as to create the sensation of walking on its surface (III-43; III-44). The different types of open or covered paths alternate unpredictably, so as to enhance the sense of surprise and contribute to the general complexity of the garden. In the same spirit, paths are often made of different materials in different sections. The choice of paving depends on the context and on the function of the paths (III-45; III-46; III-47). Some have paving of a regular design executed in bricks or smooth stones, others use irregular stones or river pebbles of different colors placed so as to compose figures.

III-43 ——

III-44 ——

III-45: Shizi lin, "Lion Grove", Suzhou. The great variety of surfaces along a path.

III-46: Yu yuan, "Garden to Please", Shanghai. The use of paving emphasizes the main garden route.

III-47: Canglang ting, "Surging Waves Pavilion", Suzhou. Black and white river pebbles are composed in a courtyard to create a geometrical pattern.

III-48: Yu yuan. Stone slabs pave a garden path by the water.

III-49: Canglang ting. A winding bridge with low balustrades over a canal leads to the entrance of the garden.

III-49

III-48

The garden designer Ji Cheng commented: "A narrow way set around with flowers is better paved with stone, while an open courtyard surrounded by buildings should be laid out in bricks… pebbles are suitable for laying on paths that are not frequently used"[4], while a paving in simple stone slabs of irregular outline seems appropriate "for paths through a mountain gully or on a slope by the water, or before a terrace or beside a pavilion"[5] (III-48). A sort of built catalogue of the many variations a Chinese garden path may take can be found in the *Canglang ting*, "Surging Waves Pavilion", in Suzhou. Here, a zigzag bridge leads to the entrance of the garden, which features a double covered walkway made of two parallel corridors separated by a wall with ornate screen windows, followed by simple covered walkways connecting the pavilions and winding around the irregularly shaped pool in a rapid succession of ramps, as well as open-air paths flanking the roofed walkways, and narrow passageways climbing the rocky mountain, winding among the rocks and penetrating grottos (III-49; III-50; III-51; III-52).

A playful contemporary interpretation of a traditional path can be found in the Red Ribbon Tanghe River Park, completed in 2008 by Turenscape (III-53). Built along the shores of the Tanghe River, which flows through the coastal city of Qinhuangdao, east of Beijing, the linear park has as its central compositional element a winding path with broad curves and slight changes in elevation. Running alongside the river walk is a continuous three-dimensional element, a big red fiberglass ribbon of solid but changing form. This ribbon serves both as seating and as a base for lighting. Its variations echo the irregularity of the path itself, and its showy red lacquer surface evokes the traditional finish of garden seats placed to facilitate appreciation of the most picturesque views (III-54).

III-50; 51; 52: Canglang ting, "Surging Waves Pavilion", Suzhou. The garden contains a sort of catalogue of paths in a Chinese Garden, including covered walkways, open-air paths, narrow passages over mountains or meandering inside a grotto.

III-53: Red Ribbon Tanghe River Park, Qinhuangdao. The park, designed 2005-2008, is traversed by a winding path which echoes the irregular riverbank.

III-54: Red Ribbon Tanghe River Park. The main route through the park is flanked by the fluid shape of a red fiberglass bench, from which the park is named.

III-54

Architectural Elements

Chinese Gardens appear dense with pavilions and buildings, but the architectural structures never dominate the overall composition. The color range of the buildings, and their airy structures trimmed with openings and latticeworks give them a quality of transparency: architecture is dematerialized; loosing its tectonic component, it is completely integrated with the garden (III-55).

The irregular forms created by rock compositions and reflecting waters establish a dialectic tension with the regularity of architectural structures. In fact, architectural elements are intended not to contrast with the garden's naturalness, but to create a complementary symbiosis through the studied elegance of their placement and their architectural forms (III-56). The siting of architectural elements in gardens is carefully considered and follows the general logic of surprise: for this reason, pavilions are hidden by trees and rocks or situated along shores or atop artificial hillocks, conforming to the idea of the garden's natural irregularity (III-57). At the same time, pavilions are special places for observing the surrounding arrangements; for this purpose their external walls are pierced by several windows, which are in turn screened by wooden latticework panels. The geometric design of the wooden panels contrasts with the natural forms glimpsed through the windows (III-58). The structures built in gardens are of diverse types, dimensions and functions, ranging from little structures for resting, meditating or simply stopping, to more elaborate architectural works, sometimes of more than one storey, for tea rooms, libraries, studies or guest-lodging.

The typological vocabulary is extensive, including the important edifices called *tang*, "halls", large buildings surrounded by porticos, with a large space in the front. *Tang* usually occupy the most central and public part of the garden, they are the places where guests were received. Other types are *lou*, "towers" of normally two stories, and *ge*, "belvederes", storied structures with open windows on all four sides. In addition to these bigger buildings, which sometimes feature wings connected by covered passageways, there are modest pavilions in protected and isolated sites away from the garden's public areas.

III-55 ——————

III-55: Zhongshan Shipyard Park, Zhongshan. Two old boat hangars peeled off to structural skeletons were transformed into lakefront pavilions.

III-56: Shizi lin, "Lion Grove", Suzhou. The crooked bridge traversing the lake features an hexagonal pavilion at the center.

III-57: Ou yuan, "Couple's Garden Retreat", Suzhou. The siting of architectural elements in the garden follows the logic of surprise.

III-58: Wangshi yuan, "Garden of the Master of the Fishing Nets", Suzhou. A group of lakeshore pavilions.

III-59: Zhuozheng yuan, "Garden of the Humble Administrator", Suzhou. Scheme of garden pavilion distribution.

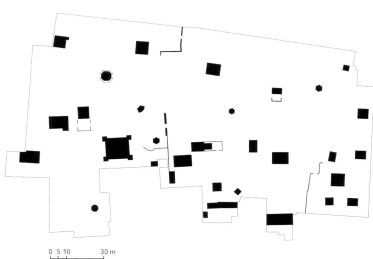

0 5 10   30 m

III-56 ——————————————————————— III-57 ———————————————————————

III-59 ——————————————————————— III-58 ———————————————————————

They can be the simple resting points from which a scenic view can be enjoyed, like *ting*, little single-storied pavilions open on all sides, or *xie*, "gazebos", which usually rise alongside reflecting pools[6]. Pagodas and other religious buildings may be part of a garden design, while memorial archways, built of wood or masonry, may mark the entry to thematic units or the beginning of a path. Terraces delimitated by balustrades, facing the bodies of water or placed on elevated points, are used as viewing points or viewing areas (III-59).

In addition to these architectural forms, Chinese Gardens present another category of structures: walls that function as internal divisions delimiting different parts of the garden. They are used to separate thematic units and to organize sequences of different scenes; and while separating them they also connect them into a visual narration by means of openings varying widely in their forms (III-60; III-61; III-62). The French Jesuit Jean-Denis Attiret wrote about this in amazement: "It was necessary for me to come here [to China] to see doors, windows of all types and shapes: round, oval, square, and polygonal of all sorts, fan-shaped, flowers, vases, birds, animals, fish, in short, any form either regular or irregular"[7]. The doorways between different parts of the garden may in fact be rounded or of complex outline, inspired by natural elements or man-made objects, as is the case of circular doors, called *yuemen*, "moon gate", or doors shaped like a vase, leaf, petal or flower (III-63; III-64; III-65; III-66). Like doors, windows have geometrical or irregular shapes, with elaborate panels or wood and stucco screens (III-67). Doors and windows are conceived as diaphragms for views, disclosing glimpses of the gardens but only through screened openings, which renders it impossible to grasp the real extension of the area they give access to (III-68; III-69; III-70).

III-60: Yi yuan, "Joyful Garden", Suzhou. A moon gate in a wave wall forms the passageway between two contiguous thematic units.

III-61: Canglang ting, "Surging Waves Pavilion", Suzhou. Doorways and windows feature complex outlines derived from natural forms.

III-62: Yu yuan, "Garden to Please", Shanghai. Windows on the wall dividing a double covered corridor; the tempting views they offer contribute to the general sense of gradual discovery.

III-63: Liu yuan, "Lingering Garden", Suzhou. A moon gate frames the view of the garden beyond.

III-64: Yu yuan. Two doors in the shape of a vase, placed in sequence, interrupt the uniformity of the rectangular corridor between two facing garden buildings.

III-65: Yu yuan. A sequence of doorways with different geometric outlines.

III-66: Shizi lin, "Lion Grove", Suzhou. A doorway in the shape of a flower frames the view of a group of sculptural rocks.

III-60

III-61

III-62

III-63 ——————————————————————————————————————— III-64 ——————————————
III-65 ——————————————————————————————————————— III-66 ——————————————

97

III-67
III-68
III-69

III-70

In gardens, but also inside homes, dwarf shrubs and trees are grown in low pots or ceramic or stone trays a few centimeters high. These are the *pentsai*, "tray plants" or "dwarf potted trees", the result of pruning young tree roots and forcing the growth of their trunks and branches. The custom came from representations of the Islands of the Immortals in the gardens, evoking mountainous islands, mythical dwellings of the semi-divine beings called Immortals, where ever more miniaturized iconic reproductions were used to create a *penjing*, "tray scene", also known as "tray landscape" (III-81). Originally these were executed with beautifully formed rock fragments placed in flat containers filled with a sheet of water to reflect the rocks. To complete the landscape effect, dwarf trees are grown on the rocks that imitate mountain peaks rising out of the sea, and moss and ferns and little shrubs and, sometimes, small figurines representing people or architectural features, complete the picture. The earliest record of miniaturized plants was found near the city of Xi'an in the tomb of a Chinese crown prince, Zhang Huai, who died in 706; the wall paintings in his tomb represent two servants in court attire, each of whom holds dwarf plants, one in a flat tray, the other in an oval bowl. The technique of miniaturization became widespread, and potted landscapes occupied prominent positions in noble mansions of the time. Gardens began to have areas dedicated to miniature landscapes. An example is the landscaped area of *Huqiu shan*, "Tiger Hill", created in the city of Suzhou in the 10th century, which even now exhibits a big collection of such compositions (III-80).

The art of *penjing* enjoyed great fortune in Japan, where it was introduced during the Kamakura period (1185-1333). The technique of *pentsai* took the name of *bonsai*, a word coming to refer to both the particular method of growing trees in flat containers and the plants themselves. In Japan, the making of miniature landscapes was not limited to a rendition of a landscape scene onto a tray. Some gardens present miniaturizations of idealized natural landscapes within their enclosures, like the Daisen-in in Kyoto, a *karesansui* garden created in 1509 as part of the large Zen temple complex of Daitoku-ji. The section along the eastern side of the main building, or *hojo*, features carefully scaled rocks and plants composed to represent a mountainous scene, with a (dry) waterfall feeding a sinuous stream flowing between islands.

1: Katherine Bedingfeld, "Wang Shi Yuan: a Study of Space in a Chinese Garden", *The Journal of Architecture* 2 (1997): 15; Valder, *Gardens*, 244.

2: Among the most sought-after are the calcareous rocks from Taihu, a large lake near Suzhou. These are big rocks of singular forms, which varied in color from white to dark grey. Sculptural and irregular, they are pierced by fissures and cavities resulting from the joint action of wind and waves. See Ji Cheng, *The Craft of Gardens*, 112-19.

3: Cao Xueqin, *The Dream*, chapter 17. http://ebooks.adelaide.edu.au/c/cao_ xueqin/c2359h/complete.html

4: Ji Cheng, *The Craft of Gardens*, 100-101.

5: *Ibid.*

6: *Ibid.*, 64-71. See also Keswick, *The Chinese Garden*, 132-135; Wong, *A Paradise Lost*, 16-18.

7: Attiret, "Lettre", 37. Translation by the author.

8: Ji Cheng, *The Craft of Gardens*, 78.

9: Peter Valder, *The Garden Plants of China* (Portland, OR: Timber Press, 1999), 186.

10: Jane Kilpatrick, *Gifts from the Gardens of China* (London: Frances Lincoln, 2007), 19. The first monograph on the orchid was written in 1233 by Zhao Shigeng, and was entitled *Jinzhang Lan Pu, Treatise on the Orchids of Jinzhang*. See Valder, *The Garden Plants*, 120.

11: See Métailié, "Gardens of Luoyang," 33-35. See also Joseph Needham, *Science and Civilization in China: Volume VI, Biology and Botanical Technology, Part 1, Botany* (Cambridge: Cambridge University Press, 1986), 394-409.

12: For a French partial translation of this work, see: Chen Haozi, *Miroir des fleurs. Guide pratique du jardinier amateur en Chine au XVIIe siècle*, trans. J. Halphen (Arles: Actes Sud, 2006).

III-80 ——————————————————————————

III-81 ——————————————————————————

IV-15: Lan su yuan, "Garden of Awakening Orchids", Portland, OR. The lake at the center of the garden, built 1999-2000, is crossed by two bridges, one of which, modeled on the Shizi lin of Suzhou, features a hexagonal pavilion.

IV-16: Liu fang yuan, "Garden of Flowing Fragrance", Huntington, San Marino, Los Angeles, CA. Plan of the garden.

IV-17: Liu fang yuan. The garden, built 2004-2008, presents five stone bridges set against a woodland of native California oaks and pine species.

1   Main Entrance
2   Studio of Pure Scents
3   Freshwater Pavilion
4   Hall of the Jade Camellia
5   Terrace That Invites the Mountain
6   Terrace of the Jade Mirror
7   Love-for-the-Lotus Pavilion
8   Bridge of Verdant Mist
9   Isle of Alighting Geese
10 Jade Ribbon Bridge
11 Pavilion of the Three Friends
12 Isle for Welcoming Cranes
13 Bridge of the Joy of Fish
14 Mandarin Duck Island
15 Pavilion for Washington

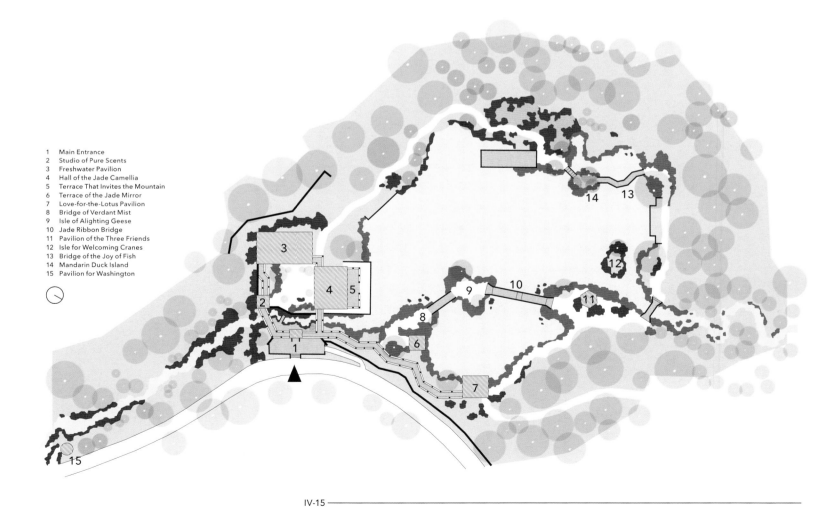

Reconfiguring the Chinese Garden

The design philosophy of all these gardens is tinged with neo-historicism. Their constant points of reference, at least in the intentions of their planners, are the classical gardens of Suzhou, which are evoked through a patchwork of diverse citations[8]. The initial motive for the adoption of these as models was the international fame of the gardens of Suzhou, eight of which – four since 1997 and four more since 2000 – are registered on the World Heritage List by UNESCO, the United Nations Educational Scientific and Cultural Organization[9]. Another factor is the role played by Chinese immigrant communities, who are often at the origin of initiatives to plant these green spaces. For these communities, the creation of traditional Chinese Gardens is a way of affirming their cultural identity and social position. From this point of view, it is perhaps no coincidence that historically-styled gardens, clearly evoking Chinese cultural identity, were created in two Chinese territories long under foreign domination: Macao and Hong Kong.

The Lou Lim Ieoc Garden, realized in the port city and former Portuguese colony of Macao in the 19th century by the local merchant Lou Kau and remodeled in 1906 by his son, Lou Lim Ieoc, was restored in the 1970s (IV-18). Conceived in the Chinese garden tradition, it is a miniaturized landscape dotted with narrow paths meandering through groves of bamboo and blossoming bushes, with a nine-turn bridge crossing a large pond filled with lotus flowers (IV-19). Similarly, in the port city and former British colony of Hong Kong in the 1970s, the Good Wish Garden was created around the Wong Tai Sin Temple (IV-20). Several pavilions, connected by covered walkways, dot the green space, which features a waterfall leaping into a pond and several rock compositions (IV-21).

IV-18: Lou Lim Ieoc Garden, Macao. The garden features a mixture of Portuguese and Chinese traditions.

IV-19: Lou Lim Ieoc Garden. The garden was conceived along the tradition of the Chinese Gardens, yet elements were emphasized to the point of seeming inspired less by tradition than by a mannered orientalism, like the nine-turn bridge in concrete meandering along a large pond.

IV-20: The Good Wish Garden, Hong Kong. Colorful pavilions joined by covered walkways are arranged around two connected artificial pools.

IV-21: The Good Wish Garden. The garden opens in the rear of the complex of the Wong Tai Sin Temple, a Daoist place of worship.

IV-20 ───
IV-21 ───

115

More recently, awareness of the historical dimension of Chinese Gardens has provoked a recovery of stylistic canons from more remote epochs. After its full return to China as a special territory, Hong Kong became the scene of the most surprising example of a neo-historical garden: the Nan Lian Garden, a public park opened in 2006 (IV-22). It is the replica of a garden of the Tang period, which lasted from the 7th to 9th centuries and is regarded by historians as a high point in Chinese civilization[10]. This little green space is an experiment in evoking the distant history of garden art. Its two rock-lined reflecting pools connected by a twisting brook make water the protagonist of the composition, and its architectural features and botanical riches are explicit reminders of Tang gardens (IV-23; IV-24).

Because most of these new gardens of historicist taste are limited in size and have been created in a cultural context far from that of the originals which inspired them, they lack that sophisticated construction typically based on the progressive unfoldment of different scenes. What prevails in them is the intent to strike the visitor through the spectacular pre-sentation of an exotic landscape, emphasized by the upward curves of the pavilion roofs, and by a profusion of moon gates. The reason for this reductive approach lies obviously in the difficulty of proposing to contemporary users, who are used to rapid consumption, a composition conceived to be savored slowly and based on elegant visual surprises.

What these reconstructions do show clearly is that the traditional garden is considered an emblematic and exportable artifact of the age-old Chinese culture. Their re-creation constitutes an efficacious demonstration of the special quality that the Chinese Garden incorporates: the joining of a refined composition, in itself a witness to history, with an attention to nature that intercepts the entirely contemporary interest in the environment.

IV-22: Nan Lian Garden, Hong Kong. The garden style developed during the Tang dynasty inspired the design of this small neo-historical public park.

IV-23; 24: Nan Lian Garden. Wooden architectural structures are arranged around two rock-lined reflecting pools connected by a winding stream.

IV-22 ⎯⎯⎯⎯⎯⎯⎯⎯⎯⎯⎯⎯⎯⎯⎯⎯⎯⎯⎯

Reinterpreting Tradition

If the neo-historical garden seems destined for further development, due also to the wider knowledge of the gardens of ancient times that archeology has uncovered, an intriguing development, parallel to but distinct from this revival of historicist taste, is the revisitation of tradition in a contemporary way. This does not imply that these contemporary gardens and parks are necessarily directly inspired by Chinese tradition. It rather suggests that some compositional elements and principles of Chinese garden design are now reconsidered as bearers of modernity, and are applied and readapted as such to contemporary landscape design. A forerunner of this design approach is the architect I. M. Pei, who in planning the open spaces for his architectural projects in China has several times included gardens that are interpretations of the classical tradition in a modern idiom. An example is the Bank of China in Hong Kong (1982-1989), or the *Xianshan* "Fragrant Hill" Hotel (1979-1982). The latter is located within the former imperial hunting grounds outside Beijing, not far from the Summer Palace, and the architect took that history into account. The hotel complex is highly articulated, with various wings built around a covered central court which contains a small rock-and-water garden (IV-25), designed by Pei himself with the close collaboration of Chen Congzhou. The meandering plan respects the presence of the old trees and also made possible the subdivision of the garden into areas with different characters, where winding paths lead through wood groves and rock-and-water compositions[11]. The biggest open space features an irregularly shaped reflecting pool at the foot of a little hill. The pool is crossed by two bridges, one of which leads to a platform on the water reminiscent of places traditionally used for poetry games. A winding watercourse is cut into the paving of the platform, in a reference to the pavilions in historical parks, where cups of wine were floated on a winding stream, called Floating Cup Stream, and the person standing where a cup stopped had to drink the wine and improvise a poem.

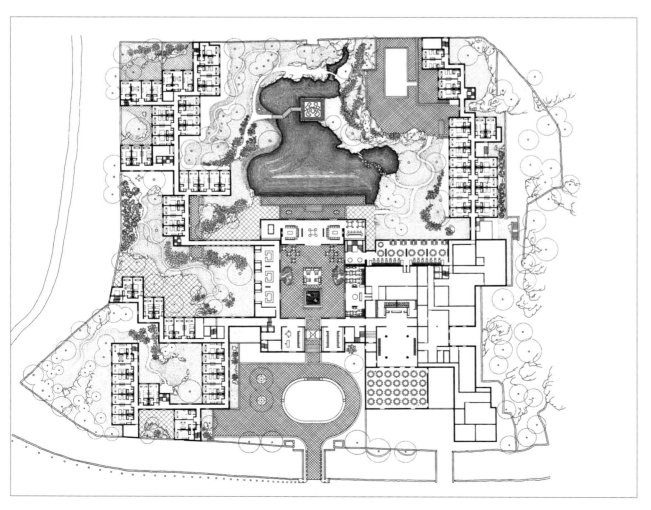

IV-25

Thus the garden respects the traditional rule of a composition in episodes, and it integrates explicit references to historical gardens without making romantic concessions: the language is generally that of the tight abstract geometry characteristic of Pei's contemporary projects. The same planning philosophy and an intense sense of abstraction inspires the project for the Suzhou Museum, completed in 2006. The organization in separate pavilions brings to mind traditional types of aristocratic residential constructions, while the use of contemporary materials like steel, glass, and cement, as well as the underlying geometry, exalted by white walls wrapped in a network of grey stone, make clear that this is a modern expression echoing tradition. The garden by Pei was created in the open space between the pavilions (IV-26). The principal element of its composition is a pool crossed by a crooked low stone walkway, which serves to connect the museum's east wing with the west one. The shores of the pond feature essential and modern renditions of traditional stylistic elements – a grove of bamboo, an open polygonal pavilion, a terrace-belvedere (IV-27). Great stone fragments emerge from the stony low northern shore, closed off by a white wall. The highly sculptural composition was inspired by traditional landscape painting, and clearly evokes hilly and mountainous scenery (IV-28).

Many gardens and open spaces created in the last decade have designs tending toward the geometrical and marked by the repetition of certain elements. These traits indicate the desire to link the new gardens and open spaces with the regularity of the urban context in which they are situated; at the same time, their plans, incisive and essential in their design, clearly speak of a sense of modernity. This decidedly new approach does not completely exclude tradition, but rather favors new forms of hybridization.

IV-25: Xianshan "Fragrant Hill" Hotel, Beijing. Plan of the complex; it was built 1979-1982.

IV-26: Suzhou Museum, Suzhou. The garden, completed 2006, is designed in a modern language of abstract geometry, which highlights the basic elements of Chinese garden tradition.

IV-27: Suzhou Museum. A grove of bamboos anticipates the main design feature of the garden, the lake.

IV-28: Suzhou Museum. A sculptural composition of rocks inspired by traditional landscape painting is set against a whitewashed wall.

IV-26

IV-27

IV-28

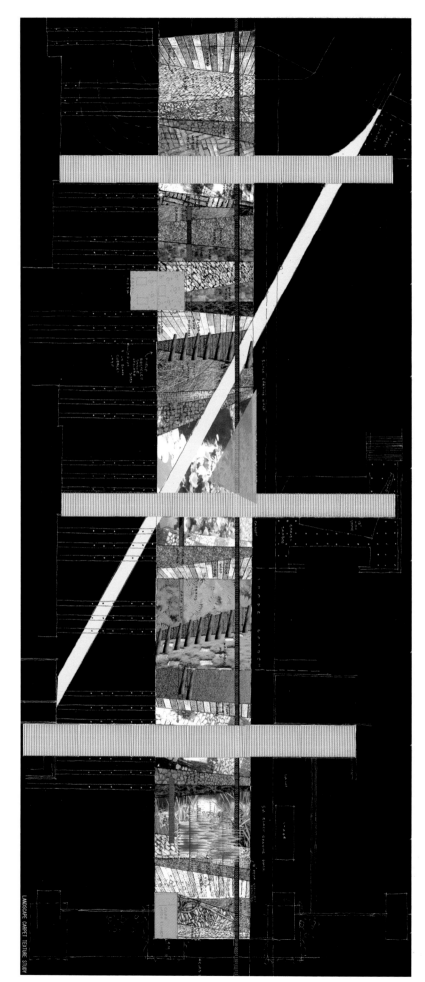

LANDSCAPE CARPET TEXTURE STUDY

IV-29: Shanghai Carpet, Shanghai. Masterplan.

IV-30: Shanghai Carpet. Model. This project was in collaboration with Skidmore Owings and Merrill LLP, San Francisco. Tom Leader Studio was responsible for the landscape design.

IV-31: City Balcony, Hangzhou. Built 2004-2008, the project was in collaboration with Obermeyer Planen und Beraten, Munich, and with ECADI – East China Architecture and Design Institute, Shanghai – who were responsible for the architecture. Jörg Michel with POLA was responsible for the landscape architecture.

IV-32: City Balcony, Hangzhou. Masterplan.

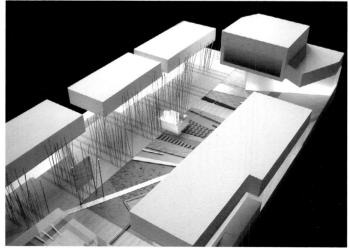

Reconfiguring the Chinese Garden

The aesthetic principle of the collection of miniature landscapes has found an original interpretation in the Shanghai Carpet (2003-in completion), a sunken pedestrian plaza designed by Tom Leader Studio, a landscape-architectural practice based in Berkeley, California, and located in Shanghai in the Yangpu district, for the University City Hub[12] (IV-29). Built over an underground parking garage, the linear composition plays with a dense alternation of planted strips and bands of different paving and material; lotus pools, bamboo groves, and intricate stone patterns evoke the alternating spaces of traditional gardens (IV-30).

On a bigger scale, an analogous inspiration lies behind the City Balcony Hangzhou (2004-2008), whose landscaping was planned by the German Berlin-based landscape architect Jörg Michel and built in an area of expansion of the city of Hangzhou (IV-32). Placed at the end of a strip lined with important urban amenities like theaters and convention halls, the balcony is a big multi-level creation facing the Qian Tang River[13]. It contains sports and recreation facilities and is covered by a great hanging garden which – functioning as a connective tissue for the new architecture of the complex – alternates irregular bands of greenery and water with different types of paving, juxtaposing a sequence of artificial landscapes with the view of the big river. Elevated glass-enclosed walkways wind their way among the buildings they connect, like the covered walkways of historical Chinese Gardens, and offer ever-changing views of the green space around (IV-31).

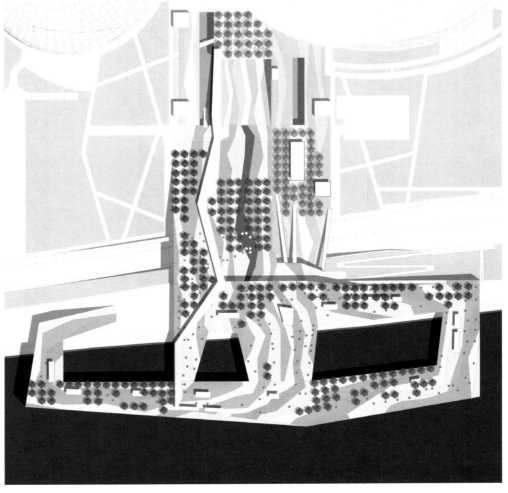

IV-31 — IV-32 —

Reconfiguring the Chinese Garden

The vernacular language of tradition takes a different turn in the Shanghai Botanical Garden in Chenshan (2005-2010), planned by a group led by the German landscape architects Donata and Christoph Valentien. The garden is configured like a closed space protected from its outside surroundings by a ring of artificial elevations, whose summit is covered by an arboretum which is punctuated by pavilions sited in correspondence with particularly scenic spots (IV-33). The central space of the botanical garden is characterized by a series of irregularly shaped ponds for aquatic plants. Emerging like islands from the surface of the water and the surrounding terrain, 37 different thematic gardens present a show of greenery boasting a high biodiversity quotient (IV-34). The vision of the garden as a space from which the outside is excluded, the contraposition of the waters and the sculptural effect of the crown of artificial hills, the presence of islands, the central position of the ponds, the general powerful dynamism of the composition, all these are elements of a design reflecting Chinese garden tradition (IV-35). But here that tradition is interpreted through the latest technologies for sustainability: a modern biological water purification system was created, and biomass and waste materials are collected and converted into energy for cooling and heating. The complex result harmonizes the didactic aims of a botanical garden with a landscape that is aesthetically pleasing and ecologically sustainable (IV-36).

IV-33: Shanghai Botanical Garden, Chenshan. Aerial perspective of the botanical garden, which was built 2005-2010.

IV-34: Shanghai Botanical Garden. The Iris Garden is one of the 37 thematic gardens spotting the botanical garden. It presents a selection of irises for dry loca-

tions, irises for moist locations and bulbous irises.

IV-35: Shanghai Botanical Garden. The large Garden for Medicinal Plants features Chinese medicinal plants at its center, surrounded by curative herbs from other countries.

IV-35

IV-36: Shanghai Botanical Garden, Chenshan. A series of irregularly shaped ponds characterize the central space of the garden.

IV-37: Paddy Rice Campus, Architectural University Campus, Shenyang. Completed in 2004, the open space of the campus is designed as agricultural fields subdivided according to a geometric pattern of quadrangular areas, which are planted with rice and other native crops.

Reconfiguring the Chinese Garden

IV-37

Sustainability and cultural identity are also the distinctive traits of the studio Turenscape's intriguing project for the green space around the Architectural University Campus in Shenyang (2003-2004), which was inspired by traditional agricultural landscapes (IV-37). The campus was built on former rice paddies, and it is precisely the geometrical landscape of these paddies that Turenscape's project evokes. A grid marks the open space, creating quadrangular pieces of different sizes, planted with rice and other native crops. Rectilinear paths, flanked in part by rows of trees, underscore the design of the rice fields (IV-38). Students are involved in farming processes and the rice produced is packaged and sold at the university or offered as a gift to visitors, thus becoming the symbol of the university itself (IV-39). This very simple composition creates a fruitful landscape that unites the conservation of the memory of the place to the current themes of local food production and sustainable land use (IV-40).

A narrative mixing local history and natural environment forms also the basis of another project by Turenscape, the Zhongshan Shipyard Park in the city of Zhongshan in southern China (2000-2002). The project aimes at the recovering of an industrial area, the site of a former shipyard. The inlet of the shipyard was reshaped into a winding lake that insinuates itself around big cranes, and the industrial structures were reduced to abstract and colorful metal skeletons, in an environment rich with flora, partly planted and partly spontaneous. Paths, which are linear but segmented, lead the visitor through different parts of the park in a play of successive revelations: green rooms, small intimate spaces for reading and relaxing, alternate with wide open spaces dominated by water whose surface reflects, like a memory of times gone by, tremulous images of the bare metal forms of an industrial past (IV-41).

IV-38

IV-38: Paddy Rice Campus Architectural University Campus, Shenyang. Sitting areas are located within the rice paddies.

IV-39: Paddy Rice Campus. Traditional agricultural practices inspired the design for the open spaces for the campus.

IV-40: Paddy Rice Campus. Sheep cut the grass, providing a fully sustainable maintenance.

IV-41: Zhongshan Shipyard Park, Zhongshan. Buildings reduced to metal skeletons, evidence of the site's industrial past, synthesize the history of the place.

IV-39 ——————————————————————————— IV-41 ———————————————————
IV-40 ———————————————————————————

Toward Sustainable Open Spaces

Sustainability is the common denominator of all recent planning experiments and will continue to inform trends in the near future. It is not alien from tradition, because the founding premises of the Chinese Garden are the same as those principles inspiring the current conception of a sustainable environment. The Chinese Garden is an ecological microcosm: it puts the visitor into an environmental metaphor, where compositions symbolizing the riches of nature are inhabited by fish and birds. The Chinese Garden is a space of balance, where people recognize without prevarication that they are an integral part of the system of nature. The Chinese Garden is also an economical construct: not only in its creation, but even more in its management. This fact was stated already more than two centuries ago by the French Jesuit Pierre-Martial Cibot, as a key motive for suggesting the Chinese Garden as an appropriate model for Europe: the rustic quality of the Chinese Garden appeared to be far superior to the very costly European gardens, which required infinite care to maintain the geometrical forms into which the greenery was forced at the time[14].

Even though the new experiments are far from the traditional stylistic canons, the contemporary turn that landscape architecture in China is taking can be considered as part of the evolution of an ancient tradition. The process has been accelerated by the anthropization of China's countryside in the last few decades, which has had a devastating impact. The widespread degradation of ecosystems has generated recent efforts in the country to recreate the natural landscape in areas sharply affected by human activities.

Kongjian Yu, founder of the Turenscape firm for landscape architecture and urban design, has experimented with processes of environmental regeneration in many of his projects, including the Yongning River Park (2002-2004), an urban waterfront park along the Yongning River in the coastal city of Taizhou, south of Shanghai (IV-42). The natural setting of the river had been destroyed by concrete embankments as a result of local flood control policy. Turenscape's task was to reconstruct the natural riverbank and the transition from the water to the urbanized area. In line with an ecological approach to flood control, the landscape architect reconstituted a riparian wetland along the floodplain, and replaced the concrete embankments which constricted the river with an earth bank consolidated with native grasses. Beyond the riparian wetland, the main park features a second and wider wetland, which connects in turn with an outer network of ponds. This wetland is crossed by paths and walkways, and features little groves of greenery and small architectural structures (IV-43).

IV-42: Yongning River Park, Taizhou. In the park, designed 2002-2004, a system of footbridges connects a network of seasonally flooded ponds.

IV-43: Yongning River Park. A square platform floats above the reconstituted riparian wetland.

IV-44: Qiaoyuan Wetland Park, Tianjin. General plan of the park, which was designed 2005-2008.

Reconfiguring the Chinese Garden

In Hong Kong, the Wetland Park (completed 2005) was planned by Urbis Limited with MET Studio Designer and created by the Special Region's Government in the New Territories, the big mountainous and well-watered wooded area beyond the metropolis, where new towns have been built in the course of the last 50 years to provide housing for immigrants. The park lies next to the most recent of the residential satellite cities, thick with skyscrapers, called Tin Shui Wai (IV-49). Construction of the city completely altered the original environment, which featured ponds and swamps offering refuge to birds along the routes of their seasonal migrations (IV-50; IV-52). The Wetland Park is a natural environment with a big visitors' center aimed at teaching the public about the ecology of wetlands. The park includes guided paths, some of them over floating walkways, which offer spots for observing the wetland biodiversity (IV-51).

In the ongoing globalization of the world, research on the local cultural as well as natural history of specific sites guides recent landscape architecture projects. The strategy seems to be to capitalize what is already there, to give a meaning to the conscious transformation of the site, and, at the same time, to reveal the beauty of the unexpected contrasts raised by this approach.

To that common pattern, to the most current international debate, contemporary Chinese landscape architecture adds the revitalization of the historical legacy as a tool to reestablish a common confidence in the long-term capability of managing the relationship with the environment. Environmental awareness melts with the Chinese Garden legacy in a synthesis of international and traditional styles.

In a country like China, which always pays attention to signs and gestures, even the creation of a garden or a park can be seen as a good auspice for the future of the country.

1: Beginning in the penultimate decade of the 16th century, the religious order of the Jesuits got established in China, aiming to introduce Christianity to that ancient, vast and well-ordered empire. The history of the Jesuits' efforts in China began in 1582, when the Italian Jesuit Matteo Ricci succeeded in establishing a mission in the Chinese empire, and ended with the suppression of the Society of Jesus in 1773 by Pope tClement XIV, whose brief officially reached missionaries in China only two years later. For the reception of the Jesuits' descriptions of Chinese Gardens in Europe see Bianca Maria Rinaldi, "Borrowing from China. The Society of Jesus and the Ideal of Naturalness in XVII and XVIII Century European Gardens", *Die Gartenkunst* 2 (2005): 319-37.

2: William Temple, "Upon the Garden of Epicurus", in *Miscellanea, the Second Part. In Four Essays* (London: Simpson, 1696⁴), 132.

3: Joseph Addison, *The Spectator* 414, June 25, 1712, quoted in Dixon Hunt and Willis, eds., *The Genius of the Place*, 142.

4: Robert Castell, *The Villas of the Ancients Illustrated* (London: by the Author, 1728), 116-17.

5: In 1763, Chambers published his designs for the pagoda in a book entitled *Plans, Elevations, Sections and Perspective Views of the Gardens and Buildings at Kew in Surry*.

6: In February 1972 Richard M. Nixon visited the People's Republic of China, where he met with Mao Zedong and other Chinese officials.

7: There are also a Japanese Garden, a Korean Garden, a Balinese Garden, an Italian Renaissance Garden, a hedge maze and a paved labyrinth symbolizing European garden art, as well as an Oriental Garden.

8: An exception to this general trend is represented by the *Yu hwa yuan*, the Chinese Garden built in Singapore in 1975, and by the Chinese Garden in Zurich, opened in 1994. The designs of both gardens evoke the character of parks in northern China.

9: Since 1997, *Zhouzheng yuan,* "Garden of the Humble Administrator", *Liu yuan*, "Lingering Garden", *Wangshi yuan*, "Garden of the Master of the Fishing Nets", *Huanxiu shanzhuang*, "Mountain Villa with Embracing Beauty", have been registered; since 2000, *Canglang ting,*

"Surging Waves Pavilion", *Shizi lin*, "Lion Grove", *Yipu*, "Garden of Cultivation", *Ou yuan*, "Couple's Garden Retreat", have been added to the list.

10: The model for the *Nan Lian* Garden was the *Jiangshouju*, a garden of the Governor of Jiang in today's Xinjiang County, Shanxi Province.

11: See Carter Wiseman, *I. M. Pei. A Profile in American Architecture* (Schaffhausen a.o.: Stemmle, 1990), 193.

12: The project was in collaboration with Skidmore Owings and Merrill LLP, San Francisco.

13: The project was in collaboration with Obermeyer Planen und Beraten, Munich, and with ECADI – East China Architecture and Design Institute, Shanghai, partners for the architecture; Jörg Michel, principal of POLA Landschaftsarchitekten, was responsible for the landscape design.

14: Cibot, "Essai", 326.

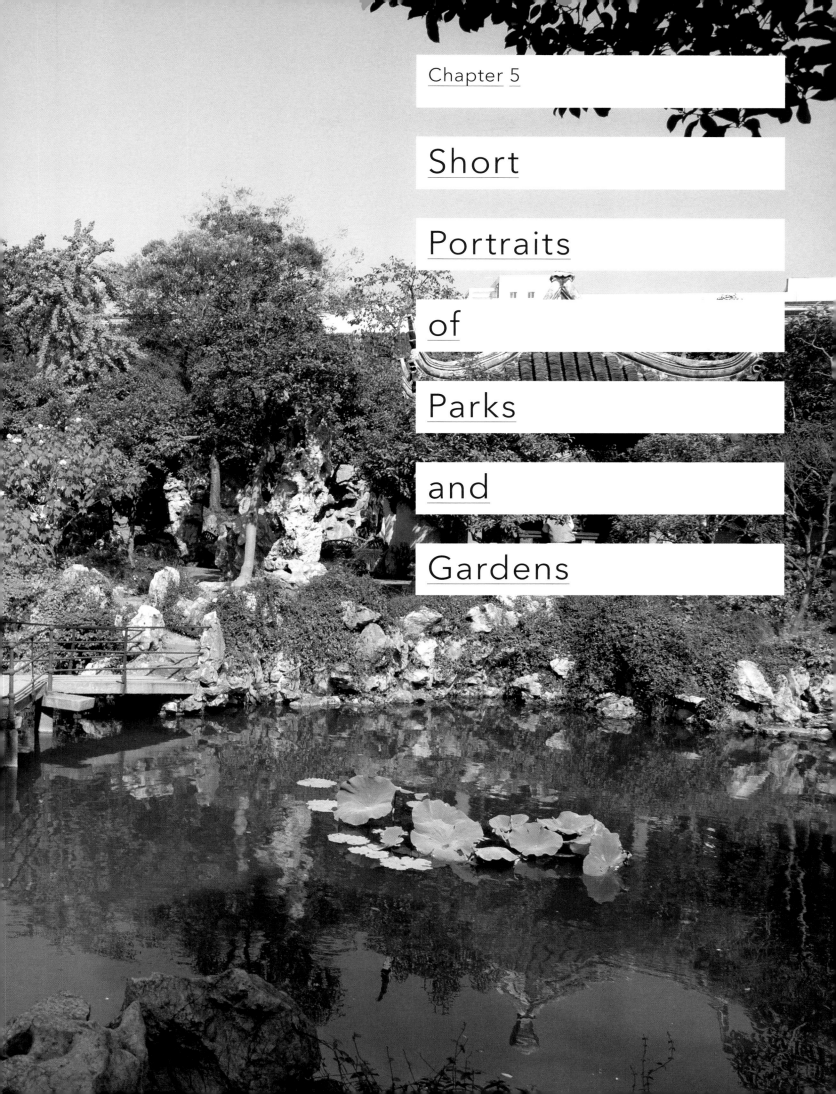

Chapter 5

Short Portraits of Parks and Gardens

This section comprises a selection of 45 parks and gardens, ranging from historical ones to most recent realizations, which are discussed as case studies within the book. All the examples have been chosen by reason of their particular features and compositional characteristics, as representatives of the design principles examined in the book. In addition to that, historical parks and gardens have been selected in relation to their historical relevance, and also because these are well preserved and accessible; contemporary projects have been selected with consideration to their compositional innovation.

The 45 parks and gardens are organized into four typological groups: Imperial Parks, Classical Gardens, Neo-historical Gardens and Contemporary Landscape Design; within each group, the sequence of the parks and gardens is arranged according to geographical location and presented in alphabetical order. The page numbers refer to the mentions of the gardens and parks in the text.

IMPERIAL PARKS

Beijing

Beihai Park

This green space, which now serves as a public garden, occupies the northernmost part of a bigger imperial park which even today embraces the entire western side of the Forbidden City. The park as a whole features a sequence of three different artificial lakes, separated by narrow strips of land. The largest, situated beyond the northwestern corner of the Forbidden City, bears the name *Beihai*, "Northern Sea"; south of it lies the *Zhonghai*, "Middle Sea", and the *Nanhai*, "Southern Sea". Out of the waters of the *Beihai* rises an island called *Qionghua dao*, "Jade Islet", because of the color of the wooded hill that covers it almost entirely. Islands also mark the other lakes (V-1).

pp. 23, *23*, 32, *33*, **33**, 136, *136*, 137

The complex, altered several times through the centuries, owes its origin to the presence of an imperial lodge constructed in the 10th century, then transformed into an imperial residence in 1179, during the Jin dynasty. An oblong lake was created near the palace, featuring a circular island with a hill. In 1266, when Khubilai Khan chose Beijing as the new capital of the empire, he had the walls of his imperial city built with the lake at the center, enriching the island with pavilions and planting the hillside with evergreens. In the Ming period, in the first half of the 15th century, the lake was expanded on the south side and radically reshaped. It was then that the existing three bodies of water were created, and gardens and pavilions were distributed along their shores. The whole complex took the name *Xi yuan*, "West Garden". But it was the next dynasty, the Qing, and especially the Qianlong Emperor, who built most of the buildings and pavilions and gardens now visible within the *Beihai* Park. In 1925, the area containing Lake *Beihai* was transformed into a large public park of about 70 ha; the remaining part of the imperial park was transformed after 1949 by the newly founded People's Republic of China into a government center, housing the Central Committee of the Communist Party of China, as well as the State Council.

Scenic sites within the *Beihai* Park evoke the gardens on canals in the southern Chinese cities of Suzhou and Hangzhou. Examples of this include the pavilions of the *Huafang zhai,* "Studio of the Painted Boats", on the northeastern shore of the lake, which face onto a quadrangular basin and are flanked by a long canal; or the *Jingxin zhai*, "Studio of the Rested Heart", an emperor's summer retreat in the northern part of *Beihai* Park, featuring a famous "garden within the garden". The garden is remarkable for the construction of its pavilions and the covered passageways which open onto irregular pools enclosed by rock formations. A white stupa, placed at the highest point on *Qionghua* Island, is the visual focus of the whole composition.

Yihe yuan, "Garden of the Preservation of Harmony"

Known as the "Summer Palace", *Yihe yuan* is today a big public park just within the northwestern stretch of Beijing's Fifth Ring Road (V-2). Its origins date back to a small palace built in 1153 during the Jin dynasty, used by the sovereigns as a residence during their travels throughout the empire. The area has changed often through the centuries, with the most important transformation taking place under the Qianlong Emperor, who in 1750 decided to expand the whole park in honor of his mother's 60th birthday in 1751. Work was not completed until 1764, however, and the park took the name *Qingyi yuan*, "Garden of Clear Ripples". With the hydrographic situation of the West Lake in the city of Hangzhou in mind, Qianlong expanded the lake at the center of the park and created two more distinct but connected bodies of water in its western part, separated by wooded strips of land; each of these three parts featured an island. The hill dominating the lake was also heightened, and numerous structures were built within the park's perimeter. The park was damaged first in 1860 by the Anglo-French troops in the Second Opium War and again in 1900 by the troops of the Eight-Nations Alliance during the Boxer Rebellion, but both times it was rebuilt by the Empress Dowager Cixi. It was following the first reconstruction that the park got its present name.

pp. *26*, **30**, 31, *31*, 32, *32*, 39, *48*, 60, 65, *74*, 81, *88*, *98*, 137, *137*, 138, *138*, 140, 156, 159

V-1: Beihai Park, Beijing. The Qionghua Island is dominated by the white stupa constructed on its highest point in 1651.

V-2: Yihe yuan, "Garden of the Preservation of Harmony", Beijing. A high octagonal pagoda on the hilltop is the visual focus of the whole composition.

V-2

The 300-ha park is centered on the harmonious juxtaposition of a hill and a big lake, both artificial. The hill, called *Wanshou shan*, "Longevity Hill", occupies the northern part of the area; densely wooded, it is dotted with temples, pavilions and gardens nestled in its intricate topography. These include the little garden called *Xiequ yuan*, "Garden of Harmonious Interest", model of a "garden within a garden", where the irregularly shaped lake is surrounded by elegant pavilions with terraces, linked by a series of paths (V-3). A high octagonal pagoda on the hilltop, the *Foxiang ge*, "Buddha Fragrance Pavilion", gives the whole park a focus. At the foot of the hill lies the big Kunming Lake, which occupies three quarters of the whole park. The lake narrows at its northwestern edge, becoming a canal at the foot of the hill. Here a landscape composition was created in imitation of a lively urban scene: two rows of low houses with shops face the canal. This is the famous "Suzhou Street", where the imperial court amused itself shopping.

In 1998 the *Yihe yuan* was added to the World Heritage List of the United Nations Educational Scientific and Cultural Organization – UNESCO.

Yuanming yuan, "Garden of Perfect Brightness"

Yuanming yuan, the "Garden of Perfect Brightness", was born as a grand complex of palaces and gardens for the sovereigns of the Qing dynasty. Situated in the northwestern outskirts of Beijing, the park was begun in 1709 by the Kangxi Emperor as a summer palace for his fourth son, the future Yongzhen Emperor. Once on the throne, Yonghzen started to expand the complex in 1725 and made it his principal residence. But it was during the reign of the Qianlong Emperor that the greatest expansion took place, making a park of over 300 ha. Qianlong added two more gardens to the original nucleus: to the east, between 1745 and 1751, he created *Changchun yuan*, the "Garden of Everlasting Spring", and to the south he commissioned *Qichun yuan,* the "Garden of Ten-Thousand Springs", whose construction began in 1772. The *Yuanming yuan* was the biggest of the three gardens and gave its name to the whole complex. It was a sort of miniature of the Chinese empire; high hills built at its western end evoked the Himalayas and a large watercourse crossing the complex represented the Yellow River.

pp. 11, 28, 30, 31, 39, 44, 47, **139**, 140

V-3: Xiequ yuan, "Garden of Harmonious Interest", within the Yihe yuan, Beijing. The small garden is one of the many features nestled in the intricate topography of the park.

V-4: Yuanming yuan, "Garden of Perfect Brightness", Beijing. Schematic plan showing the water system.

The three gardens were independent from one another yet connected through an intricate network of waterways and winding paths. Each of them featured pavilions and other structures, hillocks, valleys, groves, watercourses, rockeries, lakes, ponds and islets (V-4). The Qianlong Emperor commissioned the Jesuit missionaries, who were at the court as artists and scientific experts, to plan a further expansion of the park: a western-style formal garden called *Xiyang lou*, or "European Palaces". The team of Jesuits who took part in the project was composed of Giuseppe Castiglione, who was entrusted with the overall plan and the architecture; Jean-Denis Attiret and Ignaz Sichelbart, who designed the building details and the painted and interior decoration; Pierre d'Incarville, who took charge of the botanical aspect and landscaping; Gilles Thébault, who directed the iron work, and Michel Benoist, who managed the hydraulics, which he undertook with the aid of Pierre-Martial Cibot. Created in two phases between 1747 and 1759 in the northern part of the *Changchun yuan*, the *Xiyang lou* lay in a narrow piece of land surrounded by a wall. The Jesuits created a compendium of ornaments typical of Western gardens, including a rectangular stone labyrinth, fountains and various hydraulic devices, and an open-air theater. The various elements were presented in the form of single scenes separated by walls, in the Chinese manner. A new building was added in 1768 to display some Beauvais tapestries woven according to designs of François Boucher and presented to Qianlong by the missionaries. The European Palaces became a sort of *Wunderkammer*; Qianlong placed many gifts from European missionaries or ambassadors there, along with artifacts made by the missionaries themselves (V-5).

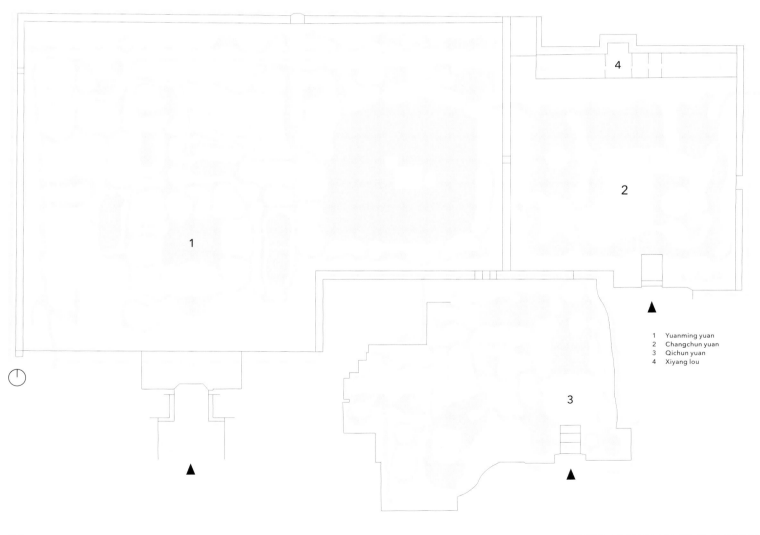

1 Yuanming yuan
2 Changchun yuan
3 Qichun yuan
4 Xiyang lou

In October 1860, during the Second Opium War, the park was first looted and then burned by Anglo-French troops. Further vandalism took place during the Boxer Rebellion in 1900. The park was partially rebuilt in the 1870s but soon dismantled to reconstruct the *Yihe yuan*, and it was never rebuilt.

Since the 1980s, the destiny of the *Yuanming yuan* has been the subject of a lively international debate over whether to protect the place as a heritage site, preserving the remains, or reconstructing it in part or completely. While no consensus has come out of the debate, in the mid-1980s one section of the European Palaces, the stone labyrinth and its central pavilion-belvedere, was completely reconstructed (V-6). In 1988 the park was declared a National Historical Relic and was partially opened to the public; some areas have undergone protective intervention and others have been examined by archeologists.

The park, both for the rich original conception and for the manner of its destruction by occupying armies, has made a strong impression on Chinese popular culture, so much so that in 1997, a miniature of part of the *Yuanming yuan* was reconstructed as part of an amusement park in the city of Shenzhen. The park has also been the subject or location of films and television series, like the successful documentary *Yuanming Yuan*, released in 2006 (produced by the Beijing Science Educational Film Studio and directed by Jin Tiemu), a mix of historical narrative with quotations from Western accounts that presents digital reconstructions of sections of the park as well as the story of its sack.

Yuhua yuan, "Back Garden of the Imperial Palace", and Qianlong Garden, Forbidden City

pp. 41n26, *77*, 140

Within a rigidly organized structure featuring a progression of palaces and great courts along a south-north axis, the Forbidden City also includes some small courtyard gardens, the largest of which is the imperial garden called *Yuhua yuan*, "Back Garden of the Imperial Palace".

Placed at the end of the Forbidden City's central axis, *Yuhua yuan* lies within a quadrangular courtyard near the Northern Gate. It was created in the 15th century during the Ming dynasty; its original plan consisted of an axial composition maintained through the following times, despite the general rebuilding which took place during the Qing period. The small green space has a walled pavilion at its center, called *Qinan dian*, "Hall of Imperial Tranquility"; the garden has a symmetrical plan, with trees in a row, regular flower beds, a collection of single rocks placed on sculpted pedestals, rectangular pools and little pavilions. Three artificial hillocks break the tight geometry of the ensemble.

Entirely different is the plan of the Qianlong Garden, sited within the *Ningshou gong*, "Palace of Tranquil Longevity". This complex, organized like a miniature Forbidden City into a sequence of palaces and courts, was built in the northeastern quadrant of the Forbidden City by the Qianlong Emperor beginning in 1771, and it was here that he withdrew in 1795 after abdicating. The garden occupies the western part of the complex and is organized around five courts, whose tone is given by stone landscapes. Rocks are placed so as to create little mountains topped by terrace-belvederes, with grottos and narrow defiles below.

V-5

V-6

Chengde, Hebei Province

Bishu shanzhuang, "Mountain Hamlet to Escape the Summer Heat"

Bishu shanzhuang, **"Mountain Hamlet to Escape the Summer Heat"**, was built as an imperial summer residence in a mountainous area about 250 km northeast of Beijing, near the city of Chengde. Situated in Hebei Province, Chengde was originally a military outpost placed on the empire's northern frontier. The Kangxi Emperor decided to transform the place first into imperial hunting grounds and then into the site of the Qing dynasty's summer palace. This choice was intended to consolidate national unity by showing favor to the people living in the border regions. Each year the Qing emperors spent a good deal of time at the resort, which became another political center for the Qing dynasty.

Construction was undertaken in several phases. In the first of these, between 1703 and 1714, the large park and its artificial lake and islands were created, as were a series of palaces and pavilions. The most significant aspects of the property at this time were depicted in a collection of 36 copper engravings made in 1712 by the Italian missionary Matteo Ripa, who was employed at the imperial court. Later in that century, during the reigns of the Yonghzeng and Qianlong Emperors, expansion and construction of more palaces and temples took place, resulting in a vast ensemble of buildings and gardens which blended harmoniously into a landscape of lakes, pastureland and forests.

Covering more than 500 ha and enclosed by a wall that ran for about 10 km, *Bishu shanzhuang* is the largest complex of imperial palaces and gardens in China. It is divided into two parts. The northwestern one is characterized by high wooded hills which cover about 80 % of the whole. In the little valleys separating the heights, numerous pavilions, gardens, temples and monasteries were created. The southeastern part of the park is flat and features, from south to north, the imperial palaces, the lake shaped into several pools and a lowland that is partly pasture, partly woods. The palaces are smaller-scale replicas of the Forbidden City, with a sequence of successive courts. The lake is divided by causeways and bridges into sections of different sizes, with several islands. Part of the flat area north of the lake was used for horse races, and the western section included a number of buildings among which stood Wenjin Hall, one of the largest imperial libraries.

UNESCO added the *Bishu shanzhuang* to the World Heritage List in 1994.

Hangzhou, Zhejiang Province

Xihu, "West Lake"

Situated west of the port city of Hangzhou, the West Lake is a large and more or less quadrangular body of water of about 6.5 km², once linked to the open sea, surrounded on the other three sides by hills. The place has always been famous for the beauty of its landscape, but it also has deep associations with Chinese poetry and literature, as well as with important personalities. In the buildings gracing the heights, it preserves the historical memory of ancient religious devotion (V-7).

V-5: Xiyang lou, "European Palaces", Beijing. Ruins of Dashuifa, "Grand Fountains", one of the structures forming the complex. Created by a group of European Jesuits for the Qianlong Emperor, the garden consisted of several scenes.

V-6: Xiyang lou. The stone maze dominated by a central pavilion-belvedere is the only section of the still-in-ruin European Palaces which underwent complete reconstruction.

V-7: Xihu, "West Lake", Hangzhou. The lake is surrounded on three sides by hills.

V-7

In the 7th century, Hangzhou became the southern terminus of the Grand Canal, the system of navigable waterways that reached all the way to Beijing. In 1127, during the Southern Song dynasty, the city became capital of the kingdom and a great cultural and economic center thanks to trade with Korea and Japan. In the same period, the shores of the lake and the surrounding hills were enriched with temples, pagodas and sacred grottos, acquiring a highly picturesque character.

To protect against flooding, the lake was given long dykes along its shores, which were planted with trees and linked with bridges, with secondary lakes beyond, making for a special landscape still admired. At the same time the lake was dredged, and the sediment was used to create islets.

The Kangxi and Qianlong Emperors of the Qing dynasty visited southern China often, stopping frequently at Hangzhou. Kangxi was the one who formulated the names of the "Ten Scenic Spots of West Lake", concise definitions of the views enjoyed in spots celebrated for the beauty of the panoramas. Those names, like "Two Peaks Piercing the Clouds" and "Moon over the Peaceful Lake in Autumn", were inscribed on stone by local authorities and placed in pavilions, which became fixed places for admiring the views.

The main body of water has three artificial islands. The principal one is called *Xiaoying zhou*, "Small Seas Islet"; it was built in 1607 and is a famous example of a water garden within a larger water garden. Even though from outside it appears to be a luxuriant green island, *Xiaoying zhou* in reality is another body of water, delimited by a curved dyke on which pavilions were built amidst a thick grove of trees. The trees make a green curtain hiding the lake within. In a play of Chinese boxes, the lake in turn has an island, rather elongated, linked to the shore by two narrow strips of land and two bridges, which divide the lake into four enclosed ponds (V-8).

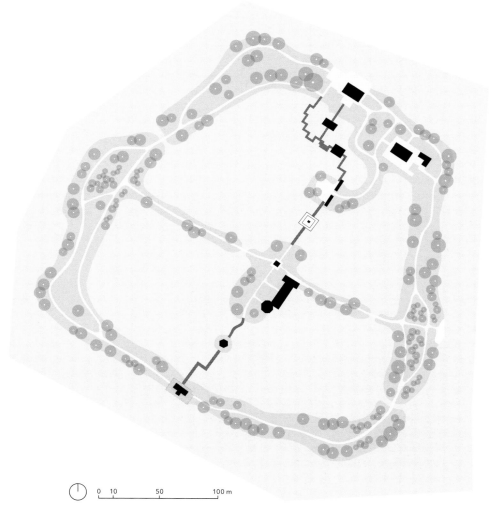

0   10   50   100 m

CLASSICAL GARDENS

Shanghai

Yu yuan, "Garden to Please"

This garden was completed in 1577 by an imperial official named Pan Yunduan, under the Ming dynasty; Pan built it for his parents as a place for them to enjoy a tranquil old age. With the decline of the Pan family fortunes at the end of the Ming period, the garden was abandoned. It was then restored in the 1760s as *Xi yuan*, the "West Garden", and its owners, a merchants' guild, transformed it into a place of business. It was at this time that a market was developed in the area southeast of the green space, and even today this part of Shanghai maintains a strong business character. During the Opium War of the 19th century, *Yu yuan* was severely damaged. Restoration began in 1956 and took five years; the garden was opened to the public in 1961. A few pavilions were recently added around the edges of the garden.

Covering an area of 2 ha, the garden has a meandering layout with a great variety of spaces, which have in common, however, an elaborated relation between rockwork and water. A large serpentine lake lies at the center of the garden, divided into two different sections by a bridge. The longer section is lined by shade trees, with compact yellow granite stones marking the shoreline; the other part of the lake features grayish white rocks of fantastic shapes along the shore (V-9). Around this central area, a series of distinct sections are connected by gates and passageways opening in the white walls that surround them. An impressive artificial mountain dominates a reflecting pool in the northwestern corner; a web of winding paths leads to a belvedere pavilion above, which enjoys a borrowed view of the Huangpu River which runs through Shanghai beyond the garden wall. To the north, two sections are divided by a narrow stream bordered on one side by rockwork set against a whitewashed wall and, on the other, by a sequence of pavilions linked by a double covered corridor. In the northeastern corner there is a broad airy paved court, with pavilions set on rockeries. The southern part of the central area is embellished by a reflecting pool crossed by a zigzagging covered walkway and a composition of three sculptural rocks evoking a mountain landscape. A sequence of paved courts flanked by a river is followed by a composition named *Nei yuan*, "Inner Garden", a small garden created next to the *Yu yuan* in the early 18th century that is now part of the overall complex.

V-8: Xiaoying zhou, "Small Seas Islet", West Lake, Hangzhou. Plan of the garden.

V-9: Yu yuan, "Garden to Please", Shanghai. Doors and passageways connect the different sections of the garden, which are separated by white walls.

V-9

Suzhou, Jiangsu Province

Canglang ting, "Surging Waves Pavilion"

This garden, apparently the oldest in Suzhou, was created around 1045, when the retired scholar Su Shunqin (1008-1048) acquired a property flanked by streams and ponds in the southern part of the city, with lush vegetation and two small hills. Su Shunqin had a solitary pavilion built there facing a canal, and it was from this pavilion that the present garden takes its name. Over the centuries the garden was used for different purposes, and only in 1695 did it become a garden again, thanks to the restoration and redesigning undertaken by Song Luo, provincial governor of Jiangsu. *Canglang ting* was never owned by any individual or family but remained a property of the local government; it functioned as a semi-public park, a place for visiting and sight-seeing. In 2000, the garden was added to the list of the UNESCO World Heritage Sites.

The main features of the garden include a big tree-covered rock-built mountain and a little lake bordered by a covered walkway with steep changes in grade (V-10). This central space is flanked on the north by a series of small sections made up of pavilions with planted courtyards and bamboo groves; a little study-pavilion rises atop a miniature rocky mountain. These sections are separated by walls punctuated with exquisite lattice screens. On the south, the garden faces a canal which, in correspondence to its southwestern corner, expands into a pond. Two pavilions connected by a covered walkway link the space of the garden and the watercourse outside.

Liu yuan, "Lingering Garden"

Located west of the historical city of Suzhou, this garden originated in a green space named *Dong yuan*, "East Garden" and was created under the reign of the Jiajing Emperor (reigned 1522-1566) for a retired official named Xu Taishi. At the end of the 18th century, the garden was owned by Liu Shu, an official who had likewise retired from public life; he enlarged the property and changed its name to *Hanbi shanzhuang*, "Cold Emerald Mountain Villa".

Short Portraits of Parks and Gardens

The next owner, Sheng Kang, bought it in 1873 and gave it the name it bears now, having made big changes by expanding it on all sides around the original nucleus with its central pool. After a period of abandonment in the first half of the 20th century, restoration of the garden began in 1953 under the Suzhou Municipal People's Government, which opened it to the public in the following year. In 1997, the garden was added to the list of the UNESCO World Heritage Sites.

The garden covers about 2.3 ha and is centered on an irregularly shaped lake dominated on the north and east by an artificial mountain with a belvedere; it is girded on the opposite sides by pavilions with wide terraces. A path crosses it and connects the two promontories jutting above the shores. Residential pavilions rise south of this central scene, and the other quadrants feature four different thematic units (V-11).

1   The Interwind Old Lake
2   Green Shade Pavilion
3   Pellucid Tower
4   Hanbi Mountain Villa
5   Osmanthus Fragrance Pavilion
6   Passable Pavilion
7   Distance Green Tower
8   Study of Enlightenment
9   Refreshing Breeze Pavilion
10 West Tower
11 Winding Stream Tower
12 Hao pu Pavilion
13 Celestial Hall of Five Peaks
14 Return-to-Read Study
15 Worshipping Peak Pavilion
16 Old Hermit Scholar House
17 Good-for-Farming Pavilion
18 Awaiting Cloud Temple
19 Cloud-Capped Pavilion
20 Cloud-Capped Tower
21 Delightful Pavilion
22 Free-Roaring Pavilion
23 Peace of Liveliness

0   5   10   20   30 m

V-10: Canglang ting, "Surging Waves Pavilion", Suzhou. A little reflecting pool, partly enclosed by a covered walkway, marks the central space of the garden.

V-11: Liu yuan, "Lingering Garden", Suzhou. Plan of the garden.

To the west, preceding a series of pavilions with small paved courts and rockeries, a larger open space features an extensive flower garden. The northeastern corner displays a collection of elevated vertical rocks of extraordinary forms rising out of a flower garden bordered by a little pool. Several pavilions face the rocks. To the north, there is a bamboo grove and a walled garden containing a collection of *penjing;* these include a rock composition rising out of a basin as an evocation of the Islands of the Immortals. Finally, to the west, there is a big rocky hill covered by trees with pavilions and a stream.

The overall composition is of great complexity in its juxtaposition of diverse thematic units, revealing that the garden was created through time with progressive additions. Nonetheless, the area around the central body of water and the portions of the garden leading up to the collection of vertical rocks offer scenes of exquisite elegance (V-12). The garden conserves notable specimens of ginkgoes around its central lake.

Ou yuan, "Couple's Garden"

Covering about 8000 m², this garden is separated by a residential complex into an East Garden and West Garden, and that coupling has given the whole site its name. The East Garden was the original nucleus, created in the 12th century by Lu Jin, a district magistrate. Its present form dates to 1874, when the garden was acquired by the governor Shen Bingcheng, who expanded it and added the West Garden, giving the complex its name. In 1941 it was bought by Liu Guojun, a textile magnate and deputy governor of the Jinagsu Province, who gave it to the city of Suzhou in 1955. The East Garden was restored and opened to the public in 1965; the West Garden was opened in 1994. In 2000, the garden was added to the list of the UNESCO World Heritage Sites.

The present entrance is through the West Garden, which features two adjacent courts with rock compositions. The larger and more open East Garden is articulated around an elongated pond, dominated by an artificial yellow granite mountain covered with trees. The pond has a zigzag bridge and is bordered by rocks and pavilions connected by covered walkways. A canal surrounds the garden on three sides and a two-storied edifice built on the southeastern corner offers a view onto the canal (V-13).

pp. *17, 26,* **27***, 28, 64, 65, 67, 95, 146, 147*

Shizi lin, "Lion Grove"

This garden was planted in a place where a temple and green space had been created by the Buddhist monk Tianru Weizi in 1342, during the Yuan dynasty, when the first great stone masses, some evoking the figure of a lion, seem to have been placed. Tradition has it that these forms recalled the mountainous area where the monk had studied, called "Lion Cliff". Rebuilt many times, modified and expanded in the course of the centuries, the garden was bought in 1917 by the family of the Sino-American architect I. M. Pei. Its remodeling lasted until 1926, and some aspects of the garden date to that period. The Pei family were the last private owners of the garden, which was opened to the public in 1954. Since 2000, the garden has been registered on the World Heritage List by UNESCO.

It occupies a surface area of 1.1 ha. The composition is a play on the pervasive presence of rocks, displaying different aesthetic possibilities in the various thematic units.

The approach to the garden is through the residential area, where a number of paved courts display single sculptural rocks. A flower-shaped gate leads to the first thematic unit of the garden proper; it is characterized by an artificial mountain made of highly irregular rocks and crossed by a web of paths which lead through grottos and up the slopes. The mountain hides a valley with a secret pavilion. A promontory extends toward the next scene, made up of a pool bordered by a sort of mountainous chain from which springs the water feeding the pool. Various pavilions look onto the pool, which is crossed by two bridges; one of them, which zigzags sharply, has a hexagonal belvedere at its center (V-14).

V-12: Liu yuan, "Lingering Garden", Suzhou. A sequence of different pavilions facing the lake.

V-13: Ou yuan, "Couple's Garden Retreat", Suzhou. Articulated around an elongated pond, the East Garden is one of the two distinct sections characterizing the garden.

V-14: Shizi lin, "Lion Grove", Suzhou. The widespread presence of rocks characterizes the garden composition.

V-13

V-14

Yi yuan, "Joyful Garden"

The garden was created at the end of the 19th century by the high official Gu Wenbin, who enclosed a portion of an earlier garden created in the Ming period. Even though it is relatively small – the garden covers only about 6000 m² – it presents a certain variety of scenes (V-15). A high, tree-covered artificial mountain, topped by a belvedere, is located in the center of a little lake of complex design, and separates two distinct thematic units, one larger and the other more intimate, both featuring pavilions facing the water. East and south of this rock-and-water composition there are two distinct sections separated by covered walkways, which present a series of green courts containing rock collections (V-16). The garden contains some remarkable specimens of loquat trees and ginkgoes planted around the central pool, as well as banana trees located in the courts.

pp. *45, 56, 74, 96, 148, 148,* **148**

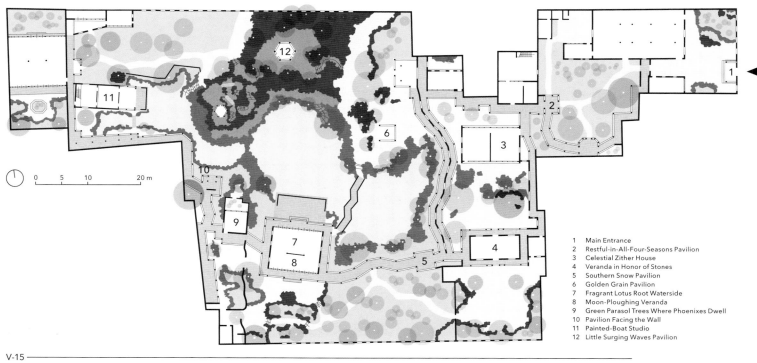

1   Main Entrance
2   Restful-in-All-Four-Seasons Pavilion
3   Celestial Zither House
4   Veranda in Honor of Stones
5   Southern Snow Pavilion
6   Golden Grain Pavilion
7   Fragrant Lotus Root Waterside
8   Moon-Ploughing Veranda
9   Green Parasol Trees Where Phoenixes Dwell
10 Pavilion Facing the Wall
11 Painted-Boat Studio
12 Little Surging Waves Pavilion

0   5   10   20 m

V-15

V-16

Wangshi yuan, "Garden of the Master of the Fishing Nets"

This garden is a refined example of how to create a complex and intricate spatial frame-work in a small space. It originated in an early-12th-century garden, created in the period of the Southern Song by the official Shi Zhengzhi. It assumed its present name in the second half of the 18th century, when it was acquired by the retired scholar Song Zongyuan (1710-1779), who redesigned it completely. In the last years of the 18th century, its next owner, the scholar Qu Zhaokui (1741-1808), modified the design yet again, creating rock-eries, planting trees, building new pavilions and restoring old ones. The garden remained in private hands until 1958, when it became public property and was opened to visitors. In 1997, the garden was named one of the UNESCO World Heritage Sites.

The 6000 m² garden is a dense sequence of green rooms and paved courtyards enclosed by wall screens, articulated around a central open space, where a continuously interrupted path follows the irregular perimeter of a reflecting pool bordered by rock compositions and pavilions (V-17).

V-15: Yi yuan, "Joyful Garden", Suzhou. The garden is centered on a little lake crossed by a zigzag bridge, with several pavilions facing the water.

V-16: Yi yuan. Plan of the garden.

V-17: Wangshi yuan, "Garden of the Master of the Fishing Nets", Suzhou. The full extent of the central pond is not visible from any one point.

17

Zhuozheng yuan, "Garden of the Humble Administrator", also known as "Garden of the Unsuccessful Politician"

The original nucleus of the *Zhuozheng yuan* was created at the beginning of the 16th century for the imperial inspector Wang Xianchen after his retirement. The long-lost original design was apparently simple and open, including few modest buildings but a great number of useful plants, including fruit trees and medicinal herbs. Abandoned at the end of the Ming period, it was rebuilt during the reign of the Kangxi Emperor. In the second half of the 19th century, it was divided into three separate but contiguous walled properties, of which the central one maintained the original name. In the 20th century, the three gardens were restored and reunited, and were opened to the public in 1952. Since 1997, the garden has been registered on the World Heritage List by UNESCO.

The garden covers an area of 4 ha. Its earlier division into three sections remains evident because of the walls crossing it, but reflecting pools, which give the garden its special character, unify the ensemble (V-18). The garden is entered from the easternmost point, which has taken on contemporary forms. Through a long wall punctuated by windows with latticework panels, the entrance opens into a small paved court enclosed by white walls. The court has a little grove of loquat trees that give the name *Pipa yuan* to this section: the "Loquat Garden". A second gateway leads to the biggest part of the complex, where an artificial lagoon is punctuated by a succession of irregularly shaped islets with various pavilions, linked by zigzagging bridges. Another wall separates another section of the garden which contains a serpentine reflecting pool surrounded by a winding covered walkway and dominated by an artificial hill, which is topped by a small belvedere pavilion. A twisting stream, whose banks are lined with rocks and low vegetation, forms a perimeter around all this, while at the westernmost edge of the complex there is a collection of *penjing*.

Yangzhou

Ge yuan, "Isolated Garden"

Probably created in the second half of the 17th century, this garden was remodeled in the 19th century for the salt merchant Huang Yingtai, who made it his private residence.

In its 5500 m² space, the garden presents four thematic units evoking the progression of the four seasons. The entrance, north of the residence, originally was through the thematic unit representing spring: bamboos and single vertical rocks fill two raised beds placed symmetrically on the sides of a moon door. This leads to the thematic unit representing summer: it is the garden's largest space and occupies its central area, with a series of

irregular reflecting pools alternating with rock compositions. The pool at the end of this sequence is dominated by a very elaborate artificial mountain of eroded limestone, topped by a belvedere pavilion. A large grotto is reached by a little zigzagging bridge crossing the reflecting pool. The unit expressing autumn, located in the northeastern part of the garden, is dominated by an artificial mountain made of yellow granite stones, traversed by a winding path shaded by maple trees, pines and cypresses. The thematic unit dedicated to winter in the southeastern part of the garden features rockeries of an especially white hue, set in a paved courtyard.

The garden conserves a bamboo collection; it is the shape of the leaves of this plant, which resemble the Chinese character "ge", which gave the garden its name.

In recent years, the garden has been enlarged considerably: north of the original nucleus a green area crossed by twisting paths has been added, and this provides a new access to the garden.

NEO-HISTORICAL GARDENS

Berlin, Germany

Garten des wiedergewonnenen Mondes, **"Garden of the Reclaimed Moon"** pp. 110, *111*, 151, *151*

The Garden of the Reclaimed Moon lies within the Marzahn Recreational Park in Marzahn-Hellersdorf, in the northeastern periphery of Berlin. The project was initiated and coordinated by producer and director Manfred Durniok, who involved various institutions: the Grün Berlin Park und Garten GmbH, Beijing Institute of Landscape and Traditional Architectural Design and Research and the Beijing Gardens and Ancient Buildings Construction Company. The garden was designed in 1994, then created between 1997 and 2000 by Chinese workers using Chinese materials.

Covering 2.7 ha, the garden displays a catalogue of typical elements of a Chinese Garden: a small lake is crossed by a zigzagging stone bridge, and there are buildings and solitary pavilions, a little waterfall over rocks, a moon-shaped door, a covered walkway, rockeries, and single vertical rocks rising out of the water (V-19).

V-18: Zhuozheng yuan, "Garden of the Humble Administrator", Suzhou. An artificial lagoon marked by a series of irregularly shaped islets and faced by several pavilions characterizes the garden design.

V-19: Garten des wiedergewonnenen Mondes, "Garden of the Reclaimed Moon", Berlin. A pavilion overlooking the reflecting pool.

V-19

Kowloon, Hong Kong, China

Good Wish Garden

The Good Wish Garden lies in the northern part of the urban area of Kowloon, in Hong Kong. It was created in the 1970s within the complex of the Wong Tai Sin Temple, a Daoist temple established in 1921. The garden features several very colorful pavilions connected by winding covered corridors, disposed around two reflecting pools fed by an artificial waterfall. A series of rock compositions complete the green space (V-20).

pp. 114, *115*, 152, *152*

Nan Lian Garden

The Nan Lian Garden is a public park located in the residential area of Diamond Hill, in the northeastern area of Kowloon in Hong Kong. It was completed in 2006. The garden occupies an area of about 3.5 ha and is a faithful replica of a Tang era garden, the *Jiangshouju*, which was part of the residence of the Governor of Jiang in today's Xinjiang County, Shanxi Province. It is organized around two separate rock-lined reflecting pools connected by a winding stream. The smaller of the two pools has an island at its center, on which stands a two-storey octagonal pavilion. Isolated vertical rocks, or groups of them, punctuate the green space.

The northern part of the garden is connected to the Chi Lin Nunnery, a large Buddhist temple originally built in 1934 and then completely rebuilt in 1990 in the style of the typical Chinese architecture of the Tang period (V-21).

pp. *18*, 116, *116*, *117*, 152, *152*

V-20

V-21

Macao, China

Lou Lim Ieoc Garden

The Lou Lim Ieoc Garden is in the heart of Macao's mainland section. It was built toward the end of the 1800s by the Macao merchant Lou Kau as part of his residence, remodeled then in 1906 by his son Lou Lim Ieoc. When the family fortunes declined, the garden changed owners several times and then became public property. After a general restoration, it was opened to the public in 1974. It offers paths meandering through groves of bamboo and blossoming bushes and is marked by rock compositions and single vertical rocks, as well as by artificial mountains. A nine-turn concrete bridge traverses a large pond filled with lotus flowers, which is fed by a high artificial waterfall (V-22).

pp. 114, *114*, 153, *153*

New York City, New York, USA

Astor Court, Metropolitan Museum of Art

Within the Asian Art collection of the Metropolitan Museum of Art in New York, the Astor Court is a Chinese courtyard garden created from the beginning of 1980; it opened to the public in 1981. The project was promoted by Brooke Russell Astor, chairwoman of the Visiting Committee of the Metropolitan's Department of Far Eastern Art and a trustee of the Museum. The design was prepared by a team of the Suzhou Garden Administration; the architects Kevin Roche and John Dinkeloo, who since 1967 had been working on the masterplan for the whole museum, implemented the plans for Astor Court. It was built by Chinese artisans using traditional methods and materials.

pp. 109, *109*, 153, *153*

Its design was strongly influenced by a small paved courtyard in the *Wangshi yuan*, "Garden of the Master of the Fishing Nets", in Suzhou. Like its model, this court has three typical garden structures: a covered walkway running along the east wall, a small main hall with a terrace which lies at the north end of the court, and an open half-pavilion along the west wall. The south wall is dominated by a single sculptural rock and four lattice windows. The courtyard is completed by elaborate compositions of Taihu rocks, plantings and a small pool intended to evoke the spring of the original garden (V-23).

V-20: Good Wish Garden, Hong Kong. The colorful pavilions are surmounted with turquoise tile roofs.

V-21: Nan Lian Garden, Hong Kong. A two-storey octagonal pavilion in the middle of a pond is the hallmark of the garden.

V-22: Lou Lim Ieoc Garden, Macao. The nine-turn bridge in concrete crosses a large pond and forms the central element of garden.

V-23: Astor Court, Metropolitan Museum of Art, New York City, NY. A glass roof covers the entire courtyard.

V-22 —————————————————————————— V-23 ——————————————————————————

Portland, Oregon, USA

Lan su yuan, "Garden of Awakening Orchids"

The *Lan su yuan*, "Garden of Awakening Orchids", is located in the heart of Chinatown in Portland. It occupies an entire city block previously used as a parking lot, covering ca. 3700 m². Work began in 1999 and the garden was finished in 2000. The garden was designed by the Institute of Landscape Architectural Design in Suzhou, with Kuang Zhen Yan as project leader and principal designer, and He Feng Chun as project landscape architect. In Portland, a local team formed by landscape architects Ben Ngan, Nevue Ngan and Associates and led by the architectural firm of Robertson Merryman Barnes supported the Chinese team. The plan was executed using traditional materials – roof and floor tiles, hand-carved woodwork, lattice windows, and over 500 tons of Taihu rocks and granite – and traditional methods, with the participation of craftsmen from Suzhou, Portland's sister city since 1988. These workers prefabricated the wooden structures in China and completed the project in Portland, adding the pathways to the garden's buildings, while the American companies of AC Schommer & Sons and Teufel Landscape were the local contractors.

A stone gateway leads into the garden, which is entirely walled in. The green space surrounds a centrally located reflecting pool, which is lined with 14 pavilions and separate spaces interconnected by winding paths. The lake can be traversed by a covered walkway and by a crooked bridge which, following the example of the *Shizi lin*, "Lion Grove", of Suzhou, presents a hexagonal pavilion at its center (V-24).

pp. 110, *112*, 154, *154*

San Marino, Los Angeles, California, USA

Liu fang yuan, "Garden of Flowing Fragrance", Huntington

Liu fang yuan, the "Garden of Flowing Fragrance", is situated within the park of the Huntington cultural institution in San Marino, in the Los Angeles metropolitan area.

It was begun in 2004 and completed in 2008, when it was opened to the public. The project was developed by a team of professionals led by He Fengchun, chairman of the Suzhou Institute of Landscape Architectural Design. A large group of Chinese craftsmen skilled in traditional Chinese construction methods, affiliated with the Suzhou Garden Development Company, constructed the garden. The architects Bob Ray Offenhauser and Jim Fry, of the Burbank-based architectural firm Offenhauser Associates Inc., were the U.S. architects of record for the project.

In its 4.8 ha space, the garden features the traditional Chinese elements: a large lake traversed by arched and zigzag bridges; two winding streams with rocky banks; simple solitary pavilions; a series of main buildings connected by a meandering covered walkway along the eastern and southern shore of the reflecting pool. A collection of rocks from Lake Tai, near Suzhou, is displayed as well. The garden's composition is dominated by thick groves of native trees, including California oaks and different pine species.

An expansion of the garden is planned, with the creation of other pavilions, a large courtyard and a covered walkway in the northern area of the green space; while in the western part of the garden a boat-shaped pavilion will be built as a viewing platform. The complex will also be enriched by a bonsai garden and a small pavilion to dominate the green space from the top of the hill southwest of the lake (V-25).

pp. 110, **112**, *113, 154, 155*

Seattle, Washington, USA

Xi hua yuan, "Seattle Chinese Garden"

The *Xi hua yuan* covers about 1.8 ha at the north end of the South Seattle Community College in West Seattle. It is a joint project of Seattle and Chongqing, its sister city in Sichuan province. The garden is divided into a sequence of different spaces: there are several paved courtyards, a mountain and two serpentine lakes linked by a rocky gorge. The composition is completed by 12 pavilions and other structures, including an education center. The garden is being completed at the time of writing; a first portion was opened in 2008, while in 2010 a second phase, with a paved courtyard, is under way. The whole project will take a total of ten years.

pp. 110, 155

Singapore

Yu hwa yuan, "Jurong Chinese Garden"

The *Yu hwa yuan*, "Jurong Chinese Garden", is in the heart of Singapore's western residential district of Jurong East. It was built in 1975 according to plans of the Taiwanese architect Yuen-chen Yu, as part of a larger recreational development, organized around a big body of water called the Jurong Lake, and including a Japanese Garden and the Jurong Bird Park. The 13-ha garden occupies one of the irregularly shaped islands marking the lake. Unlike many other Chinese Gardens built outside China, which are inspired by the classical gardens of Suzhou, the design of the *Yu hwa yuan* evokes the character of parks in northern China: the broad bridge sustained by asymmetrical arcades, which offers access to the

pp. 133n8, 155

V-24: Lan Su Yuan, "Garden of Awakening Orchids", Portland, OR. Nestled in the Chinatown neighborhood of the Old Town, the garden design was inspired by the classical Chinese Gardens spotting the city of Suzhou.

V-25: Liu Fang Yuan, "Garden of Flowing Fragrance", Huntington, San Marino, Los Angeles, CA. Traditional elements of Chinese garden design are merged into dense groves of local vegetation.

garden, is inspired by the Seventeen-Arch bridge in the *Yihe yuan* imperial park, near Beijing, while the design of the four pavilions built in the green space is based on the style of northern Chinese pavilions. The seven-storey pagoda atop an artificial hill has a configuration like that of the Linggu Pagoda, built in 1929 on the grounds of the Buddhist Linggu Temple, in Nanjing.

In 1992, the *Yun xiu yuan*, "Penjing Garden", was added to the complex, characterized by a series of walled courtyards in which are displayed examples of *penjing*.

Sydney, New South Wales, Australia

Garden of Friendship

The Garden of Friendship lies at the southern end of Darling Harbour, on the edge of Chinatown, in Sydney. It celebrates the sister-state relationship between the southern China province Guangdong and New South Wales. The design was created by the Guangdong Landscape Bureau in Sydney's sister city, Guangzhou, as a joint government project to be undertaken by a combination of Chinese and Australian craftspeople and artisans. Local consultants completed the planning, the detailed design and documentation of all elements within the garden: the Sydney-based architecture firm Tsang & Lee prepared architectural documentation for buildings and pavilions; the documentation for the landscape elements was executed by EBC Consultants. Its construction was begun in 1986, and the garden was inaugurated in 1988 as part of the celebrations for the bicentennial of the foundation of the city of Sydney.

pp. *100, 103,* 109, *109, 110,* 156, *156*

One ha in extent, it is one of the biggest neo-historical gardens built outside China. The garden presents a sequence of episodes: a mountain, two waterfalls, a rushing brook, a bamboo grove, all linked by paths girdling the big central lake, which is crossed by zigzagging bridges. Various pavilions are immersed in the vegetation, and single vertical rocks arise here and there. A twin pavilion with a double roof erected along the shore of the lake symbolizes the friendship and cooperation between Guangdong province and New South Wales (V-26).

V-26: Garden of Friendship, Sydney. The twin pavilion symbolizes friendship and collaboration between Guangdong province and New South Wales.

Vancouver, British Columbia, Canada

Dr. Sun Yat-Sen Classical Chinese Garden

Named after the revolutionary leader and first president of the Republic of China, Dr. Sun Yat-Sen (1866-1925), this garden sits in the heart of Vancouver's Chinatown. It was begun in 1985, with both craftsmen and materials imported from China, and finished in 1986 in time for the Expo 86 in Vancouver.

pp. 109, 157

The garden covers an area of about 1000 m². Inspired by the classical gardens of Suzhou, it features a little reflecting pool at its center, surrounded by various spaces linked by winding paths. Rockeries and individual vertical rocks rise here and there throughout the green space. A pavilion atop an artificial hill creates a visual point of reference for the whole composition.

The little garden was built next to a bigger public park, also neo-historical in composition, the Dr. Sun Yat-Sen Park, completed in 1983 as part of the nearby Chinese Cultural Center. The two green spaces are connected by the artificial lake and separated by a zigzagging double covered walkway. The park is organized around the larger section of the lake. Crossed by various bridges, it features at its center an hexagonal pavilion built on a little, flat, rocky island, while the main buildings are arranged along the shores.

The project for the garden and the park was conceived as a whole. The overall plan was designed in Vancouver and resulted from the collaboration between a team of the Suzhou Garden Administration – led by Zhang Bao-rong, with Wang Zu-Xin as chief architect, and with Zhou Guan-Wu, Feng Xiao-Lin and Yao Ba-Sun –, the Vancouver-based landscape architect Don Vaughan and the Vancouver-based architect Joe Y. Wai, who was also chief architect for the garden and park.

CONTEMPORARY LANDSCAPE DESIGN

Beijing

Beijing Olympic Green (Olympic Central Area and Olympic Forest Park)

The Beijing Olympic Green is a combination of two urban parks formed on the occasion of the Olympic Games; it was completed in 2008. Located on the northern extension of the historical city's central axis, it is the green backbone of a vast urban expansion and transformation of Beijing's periphery. It consists of the Olympic Central Area, the new urban linear park alongside the Olympic venues, and the Olympic Forest Park, which closes the Olympic area to the north.

pp. 34, *35*, **36**, 37, *37*, 39, 41n28, **46**, 47, *65*, 79, *80*, *86*, 157-158, *158*

The masterplan for the Olympic Green was first prepared by Sasaki Associates Inc., an interdisciplinary design and planning firm based in Boston and San Francisco. In 2002, the company won the international competition for the conceptual planning and design of the area, and it was further developed in collaboration with the Beijing Tsinghua Urban Planning & Design Institute. In 2004-2005 a large team led by chief designer Hu Jie, director of the Planning & Design Branch of Landscape Architecture, Beijing Tsinghua Urban Planning & Design Institute, Tsinghua University (Beijing), finished the establishment of the Olympic Forest Park.

The Olympic Central Area was designed by another team comprising several companies and institutions. It is organized around a winding stream that flows to the north into a lake at the center of the Olympic Forest Park, whose shape evokes a dragon's head. The Olympic Forest Park constitutes a filter between the urban areas and the peripheral areas of Beijing. It covers an area of 650 ha and is divided by the distinctive Fifth Ring Road, a super-highway which traverses it from east to west. The southern part of the Olympic Forest Park, which is connected to the Olympic Central Area, is organized around the big lake and has a more urban character; here you find diverse educational and recreational facilities, a large paved piazza, children's playgrounds, an open-air theater and exhibition centers, all immersed in an ecosystem made of woods and wetlands (V-27). A steep rocky hill was created behind the lake. The northern part of the park has a more natural character which preserves the local biodiversity. An ecological corridor crosses the Fifth Ring Road and links the two areas of the park, facilitating migration of various animal species. A sophisticated self-sustaining and self-regulating water system was created. It is made of a network of streams, lakes and wetlands and is based on the reclamation and reuse of grey water, surface runoff, rain and flood water. An ecological purification system was built using constructed wetlands as natural water filter. (V-28). The Olympic Forest Park won a 2009 Honor Award of the American Society of Landscape Architects – ASLA.

V-27

Short Portraits of Parks and Gardens

Garden of the *Xianshan* ("Fragrant Hill") Hotel

The *Xianshan* ("Fragrant Hill") Hotel, designed by I. M. Pei & Partners and completed in 1982, is located within a former imperial hunting grounds outside Beijing, not far from the *Yihe yuan*, "Garden of the Preservation of Harmony", which is now a large public park. The hotel complex is made up of various wings which extend out from a central open court with a small rock-and-water garden. The different parts of the building, which follow a meandering plan, subdivide the garden into areas with distinctive characteristics, where paths wind among compositions of wood, rocks and water. The main open space is in the southern part of the complex, near the most private area of the hotel, with an irregularly shaped lake crossed by two short bridges. The bigger of the two leads to a platform over the water; the floor of the platform is crossed by a curving channel, a citation of a cup-floating stream, which is a peculiarity of historical garden design in China, linked to friendly poetry contests.

pp. 118, **118**, 159

Hangzhou, Zhejiang Province

City Balcony Hangzhou

City Balcony Hangzhou was designed by a team made up of the Berlin-based landscape architect Jörg Michel, who was responsible for the landscape design, and Obermeyer Planen und Beraten of Munich with ECADI – East China Architecture and Design Institute of Shanghai, in charge of overall planning and the architecture of the buildings. Designed and built 2004-2008, it is located in the southern part of the city of Hangzhou along the northern shore of the Qian Tang River, where it forms part of a series of interventions of urban transformation for the new central district of Qiangjiang.

Situated at the end of a green strip along which were positioned some important new urban structures, theaters and convention halls, the City Balcony is a big multi-storey structure facing the river, a complex of green plazas and promenades on various levels, which function as connective tissue for the building works of the complex (V-29). It contains sports facilities and parking garages, and the facades are covered by a hanging garden, alternating irregular bands of planting, water and paving, thus juxtaposing a series of artificial landscapes all with a view of the big river.

pp. 121, *121*, **121**, 159, *159*

V-27: Olympic Forest Park, Beijing. The south main entrance to the park is organized around a plaza and features a distinctive urban character.

V-28: Olympic Forest Park. The program of the whole park is based on an ecologically sustainable design.

V-29: City Balcony, Hangzhou. The urban space alternates curving bands of planting, water and paving.

29

Hong Kong

Bank of China

The Bank of China Tower, built between 1985 and 1989 by I. M. Pei & Partners and opened in 1990, is located at No.1 Garden Road, in Hong Kong's business and financial core. The building is characterized by four prism-shaped shafts of glass and steel, which tower 70 stories above the ground floor level.

The building is surrounded on three sides by a rock-and-water garden, which integrates the geometry of the triangular lines that make up the profile of the sharp-edged tower. Designed by Pei himself from 1982 onwards and completed in the same year as the building, the garden covers 1300 m² on several levels, following the steep topography of the site.

In its highest part, corresponding to the main entrance to the bank's lobby, the garden opens onto a calm reflecting pool featuring golden carps; the whole water composition begins here, branching out into two angular terraced basins below, situated along the opposite sides of the building. The basins respond to the sloping site by using a small number of compositional elements that are organized in a variety of ways: triangular grey granite slabs and big single rocks interrupt the water streaming down, creating a series of little waterfalls, which feed various pools (V-30).

pp. 34, **34**, *35*, 49, *49*, 118, 160, *161*

Wetland Park

Located in the New Territories and completed in 2005, the Wetland Park is a naturalistic park created as a refuge for migrating birds, to compensate for a substantial loss of wetland habitats caused by large-scale housing and urban development. The project team included: the firm Urbis Limited, as landscape architects; MET Studio Design, as exhibition designers; and the Architectural Service Department of the HKSAR (Hong Kong Special Administrative Region) Government. Covering 61 ha, the Wetland Park shelters a series of wildlife habitats ideal for various species of migrating birds: marsh, reed bed, fishpond, wet woodland and wetland agricultural fields were created to maximize biodiversity. The park includes a large visitor center, located near the main entrance, as well as exhibition and educational facilities focusing on the themes of sustainable development, protection of the environment and wetlands conservation. Guided paths, including floating walkways, traverse the various areas of the complex, marked here and there by blinds for bird-watching (V-31).

pp. *132*, 133, 160, *160*

V-46

Tieling, Liaoning Province

Lotus Lake Wetland Park

The goal of re-creation of a natural landscape in an area transformed by agricultural use, and of construction of habitats for diverse species of migrating birds, inspired the plan of the Lotus Lake Wetland Park in the northeastern Chinese city of Tieling. Planned by landscape architects Hu Jie and Yixia Wu, along with the engineers Lushan Lu and Yi Han, the park was completed in 2009.

The park lies under the East Asian Flyway of Migratory Birds on a site that was originally wetlands and ponds but which had been altered by intense agricultural use. It was created around a big pre-existing lake which was extended on the south and east by a sequence of smaller bodies of water. Three low islets in the lake's center offer safe and isolated breeding areas for birds.

A hill, covered with a great variety of trees and bushes, flanks the main lake on the south; it welcomes singing birds, wild birds and land birds and functions as a barrier between the city and the rest of the park. North of the lake, a new wetlands area has been created for water birds and shore birds, completing the park in that direction. There are simple paths crossing the park and tiny structures for bird-watching (V-45). The project won second place at the 2009 International Torsanlorenzo Prize.

pp. 130, **130**, *131*, 170, *171*

Zhongshan, Guangdong Province

Zhongshan Shipyard Park

The Zhongshan Shipyard Park resulted from the transformation of a highly polluted former shipyard in use from the 1950s until 1999. It is located in the central district of Zhongshan, a city which lies south of the Pearl River Delta.

Designed by Turenscape in 2000-2001 and completed in 2002, the new park occupies 11 ha around the shipyard harbor, transformed into a lake along whose twisting shores different sections of the park were created: the Green Rooms, small intimate spaces for reading and relaxing, the Red Box, a room for contemplation enclosed by a red steel wall, the Ecological Island, created to protect a group of pre-existing banyan trees, and an art museum, all of which alternate with big open spaces dominated by the water. Linear but segmented paths link the different sections in a play of progressive revelations (V-46).

Evidence of the site's industrial past – buildings reduced to metal skeletons, painted in brilliant colors, train tracks which form part of the network of paths, big cranes for raising ships that mark the park's entrances as giant totems – synthesizes the history of the place. The project won a 2002 ASLA Honor Award.

pp. 44, *44*, 68, *94*, 126, *127*, 170, *171*

V-47: Lotus Lake Wetland Park, Tieling. The park was created along a pre-existing and now enlarged lake.

V-48: Zhongshan Shipyard Park, Zhongshan. A former shipyard has been transformed into a public park.

APPENDIX

ON THE AUTHOR

Bianca Maria Rinaldi is Assistant Professor of Landscape Architecture at the School of Architecture and Design at Ascoli Piceno, University of Camerino, Italy, which she joined in 2010, and co-editor of *JoLA - Journal of Landscape Architecture*.

She received a degree in Architecture from the University of Camerino in 2000 and a Ph.D. in Landscape Architecture from the Leibniz University of Hanover, Germany, in 2004. She has been a Research Fellow at the CGL_Centre for Garden Art and Landscape Architecture of the University of Hanover from 2002 until 2004.

Her previous faculty appointments were as Assistant Professor (Universitätsassistentin mit Doktorat) of Landscape Architecture at the Institute for Landscape Architecture, University of Natural Resources and Applied Life Sciences in Vienna, Austria, where she taught from 2005 until 2008, and at the Institute for Architecture and Landscape, School of Architecture, Graz University of Technology in Graz, Austria, from 2009 until 2010. She has taught courses in history and theory of landscape architecture as a visiting faculty member at the National University of Singapore (2010).

She is the author of *The 'Chinese Garden in Good Taste'. Jesuits and Europe's Knowledge of Chinese Flora and Art of the Garden in 17th and 18th Centuries* (2006) and numerous other book chapters and articles published in scholarly journals, including the *Journal of Landscape Architecture* and *Die Gartenkunst*.

Her scholarly studies focus on both historical and contemporary landscape architecture with an emphasis on Far East Asia; on cross-cultural influence in landscape architecture; and on the history and criticism of landscape architecture.

ACKNOWLEDGMENTS

Many people and institutions were instrumental in making this book possible and I am delighted to express my gratitude here.

My travels to China began in Hanover, Germany. I want to thank first of all the Centre for Garden Art and Landscape Architecture (CGL) at Leibniz University of Hanover, which accepted me as a research fellow in 2002 and gave me the possibility to begin my studies of the Chinese Garden. A sincere thanks goes to Joachim Wolschke-Bulmahn; I have been fortunate to receive his advice and his constant encouragement.

In Beijing, I had the opportunity to give a lecture during the international conference in 2008 on *Interaction and Exchange at the Court: Westerners and the Qing (1644-1911)*, in the extraordinary setting of the *Yuanming yuan* park. For this I want to acknowledge the Ricci Institute for Chinese-Western Cultural History of the University of San Francisco, the Beijing Renmin University and The Beijing Center for Chinese Studies.

I owe Franco Panzini more than simple gratitude for his foreword to this book. He gave me full access to his incredible photographic archive and also offered careful reading of the manuscript, providing key criticisms and thoughtful suggestions which have significantly improved this book's content. For all this, and also for the inspiration and guidance through the years I'm truly grateful.

A warm thanks goes to Udo Weilacher, who introduced me to the Birkhäuser publishing house.

I am very grateful to Eva Berger, Gisla and Tito Conforti, Barringer Fifield, Hubertus Fischer, Gert Gröning, Feng Han, Minghui Hu, Kelly Shannon, Marc Treib, Kathy Gibler, Hanna B. Thompson, Nathan Jay and Wayne Johnson; they all provided precious information, assistance, suggestions, and stimulating discussions at various stages. A much-felt thanks to Doretta Rinaldi and Alessandro Santoriello for illuminating technical counsel on graphic design.

I am profoundly thankful to all the landscape architects, architects and artists who made an invaluable contribution to this book by generously giving information and extensive sets of photographic and graphic material about their projects and by allowing these to be reproduced, as well as by patiently answering all my questions. I would like to thank: Pei Cobb Freed & Partners and their photo archivist James Balga; Kongjian Yu; Hu Jie; Ai Weiwei; Jörg Michel; Iwan Baan; Tom Leader and Elizabeth Kee; Donata and Christoph Valentien, as well as the whole team responsible for the design of the Shanghai Botanical Garden in Chenshan: Straub+Thurmayr Landscape Architects and Auer+Weber Architects; I would like also to acknowledge Jan Siefke and Klaus Molenaar, authors of some photos of the Shanghai Botanical Garden published in this book.

I also wish to gratefully acknowledge the cooperation of some institutions which have kindly supplied me with significant images and have allowed their publication: The Huntington Library, Art Collection and Botanical Gardens in San Marino, California; the Lan Su Yuan Chinese Garden in Portland, Oregon; the Freer Gallery of Art and Arthur M. Sackler Gallery, Smithsonian Institution in Washington, D.C.; the Palace Museum in Beijing; the Shanghai Museum in Shanghai; the Bibliothèque nationale de France in Paris.

It is a great pleasure to thank the editor for the publisher, Andreas Müller, for his expert guidance and his assistance through the different phases of this project; Reinhard Steger, for the great care he gave to the layout; Michael Wachholz for meticulous proofreading. They were a wonderful team to work with.

Initial work on this book, in 2009, coincided with the beginning of my time at the School of Architecture at the Graz University of Technology; I want to thank all my colleagues at the Institute for Architecture and Landscape for their affectionate welcome and the collegial atmosphere they created. In addition, I wish to acknowledge the friendly assistance of the staff at the University Library of the Graz University of Technology.

The final phases of the book were completed in Italy at the School of Architecture and Design at Ascoli Piceno, University of Camerino; I would like here to render a sincere thanks to its director, Umberto Cao.

Finally, I would like to thank my parents for having been so wonderfully supportive of this enterprise.

BIBLIOGRAPHY

The following bibliography lists selected studies in Western languages. For a comprehensive, topically ordered bibliography of 20th century studies, including texts in Western languages as well as works in Chinese and Japanese, refer to:
Fung, Stanislaus. "Guide to secondary sources on Chinese gardens". *Studies in the History of Gardens & Designed Landscapes* 18, 3 (1998): 269-286.

For on-line bibliographical resources on gardens in China refer to the bibliography compiled by François Louis, Bard Graduate Center, New York, NY: http://inside.bard.edu/~louis/gardens/bibliochinaalpha.htm , accessed Dec. 6, 2010

Contributions of the *Journal of Chinese Landscape Architecture* in English can be found under the following link: http://en.cnki.com.cn/Journal_en/C-C038-ZGYL-2010-11.htm (current vol., accessed 8 Feb 2011)

History of the Chinese Garden

Baud-Berthier, Gilles and Sophie Couëtoux and Che Bing Chiu, eds. *Le Jardin du lettré: Synthèse des arts en Chine*. Besançon: Les Éditions de l'Imprimeur, 2004.

Cheng, Liyao. *Ancient Chinese Architecture: Imperial Gardens*. Vienna-New York: Springer, 1998.

Cheng, Liyao. *Ancient Chinese Architecture: Private Gardens*. Vienna-New York: Springer, 1999.

Chiu, Che Bing. *Jardins de Chine ou la quête du paradis*. Paris: Editions de La Martinière, 2010.

Fang, Xiaofeng. *The Great Gardens of China: History, Concepts, Techniques*. New York: Monacelli Press, 2010.

Hargett, James M. "The Pleasure Parks of Kaifeng and Lin'an during the Song (960-1279)". *Chinese Culture* 30, 1 (1989): 61-78.

Lou, Qingxi. *Chinese Gardens*, Beijing, China Intercontinental Press, 2003.

Qian, Yun, ed. *Classical Chinese Gardens*. Hong Kong: Joint Publishing Company Ltd., 1982.

Shi, Mingzheng. "From Imperial Gardens to Public Parks: The Transformation of Urban Space in Early Twentieth-Century Beijing". *Modern China* 24, 3 (1998): 219-254.

Stuart, Jan. "Ming dynasty gardens reconstructed in words and images". *Journal of Garden History* 10, 3 (1990): 162-172.

Studies in the History of Gardens & Designed Landscapes, Chinese Gardens I, 18, 3 (1998).

Studies in the History of Gardens & Designed Landscapes, Chinese Gardens II, 19, 3/4 (1999).

Turner, Tom. *Asian Gardens: history, beliefs and design*. Abingdon, New York: Routledge, 2010.

Valder, Peter. *Gardens in China*. Portland, Oregon: Timber Press, 2002.

Xu, Yinong. *The Chinese City in Space and Time. The Development of Urban Form in Suzhou*. Honolulu, Hawai'i: University of Hawai'i Press, 2000.

Xu, Yinong. "Gardens as a Cultural Memory in Suzhou, Eleventh to Nineteenth Centuries". In *Gardens, City Life and Culture: A World Tour*, edited by Michel Conan and Chen Wangheng, 203-228. Cambridge, Massachusetts: Harvard University Press, 2008.

Chinese Garden Design and Composition

Bedingfeld, Katherine. "Wang Shi Yuan: a Study of Space in a Chinese Garden". *The Journal of Architecture* 2 (1997): 11-41.

Chen, Congzhou. *On Chinese Gardens*. Translated by Chen Xiongshan et al., New York: Better link press, 2008.

Clunas, Craig. *Fruitful Sites. Garden Culture in Ming Dynasty China*. London: Reaktion Books, 1996.

Feng, Jin. "*Jing*. The Concept of Scenery in Texts on the Traditional Chinese Garden: An Initial Exploration". *Studies in the History of Gardens & Designed Landscapes* 18, 4 (1998): 339-365.

Fung, Stanislaus. "Movement and Stillness in Ming Writings on Gardens". In *Landscape Design and the Experience of Motion*, edited by Michel Conan, 243-262. Washington, D.C.: Dumbarton Oaks, The Trustees for Harvard University, 2003.

Gournay, Antoine. "L'aménagement de l'espace dans le jardin chinois". In *Asies 2, Aménager l'espace*, edited by Flora Blanchon, 263-279. Paris: Presses de l'Université de Paris-Sorbonne, 1994.

Gournay, Antoine. "Le système des ouvertures dans l'aménagement spatial du jardin chinois". *Extrême-Orient, Extrême-Occident, L'art des jardins dans les pays sinisés* 22 (2000): 51-71.

Gournay, Antoine. "Chine: jardins du Lingnan à la fin de la dynastie des Qing". *Polia* 1 (2004): 63-78.

Harrist, Robert E. "Site Names and their Meaning in the Garden of Solitary Enjoyment". *Journal of Garden History* 13 (1993): 199-212.

Harrist, Robert E. "Mountains, Rocks and Stone Pictures: Forms of Visual Imagination in China", *Orientations* 34, 10 (2003): 39-45.

Hu, Dongzhu. *The way of the virtuous: the influence of art and philosophy on Chinese garden design*. Beijing: New World Press, 1991.

Ji, Cheng, *Yuanye, le Traité du jardin. 1634*. Translated by Che Bing Chiu. Besançon: Les Éditions de l'Imprimeur, 1997.

Ji, Cheng, *The Craft of Gardens - Yuan ye*. Translated by Alison Hardie. New Haven, Connecticut: Yale University Press, 1988.

Johnston, Stewart R. *Scholar Gardens of China. A study and analysis of the spatial design of the Chinese private garden*. Cambridge, Massachusetts: Cambridge University Press, 1991.

Keswick, Maggie. *The Chinese Garden. History, art and architecture*. London: Frances Lincoln, 2003[2].

Kilpatrick, Jane. *Gifts from the Gardens of China*. London: Frances Lincoln, 2007.

Makeham, John. "The Confucian role of names in traditional Chinese gardens". *Studies in the History of Gardens & Designed Landscapes*, Chinese Gardens I, 18, 3 (1998): 187-210.

Métailié, Georges. "Some hints on 'Scholar Gardens' and plants in traditional China". *Studies in the History of Gardens & Designed Landscapes* 18, Chinese Gardens I, 3 (1998): 248-256.

Métailié, Georges. "Gardens of Luoyang: The Refinements of a City Culture". In *Gardens, City Life and Culture: A World Tour*, edited by Michel Conan and Chen Wangheng, 31-39. Cambridge, Massachusetts: Harvard University Press, 2008.

Sensabaugh, David A. "Fragments of Mountain and Chunks of Stone: The Rock in the Chinese Garden". *Oriental Art* 44, 1 (1998): 18-27.

Sensabaugh, David A. "A Few Rocks Can Stir the Emotions: Chinese Gardens and Scholars". *Orientations* 31, 1 (2000): 32-39.

Sirén, Osvald. *Gardens of China*. New York: Ronald, 1949.

Tsu, Frances Ya-sing. *Landscape design in Chinese gardens*. New York: McGraw-Hill, 1988.

Valder, Peter. *The Garden Plants of China*. Portland, Oregon: Timber Press, 1999.

Wang, Yi. "Interior display and its relation to external spaces in traditional Chinese gardens". *Studies in the History of Gardens & Designed Landscapes*, Chinese Gardens I, 18, 3 (1998): 232-247.

Yang, Hongxun. *A treatise on the gardens of Jiangnan. A study into the classical art of landscape design of China*. Translated by Xue Manjuan. Shanghai: Shanghai People's Publishing House, 1994.

Yang, Hongxun. *The Classical Gardens of China. History and Design Techniques*. New York: Von Nostrand Reinhold, 1982.

Zhou, Hui. "The *jing* of a perspective garden". *Studies in the History of Gardens & Designed Landscapes*, 22, 4 (2002): 293-326.

Individual Chinese Gardens and Gardens of Specific Regions

Berliner, Nancy. *Juanqinzhai in the Qianlong Garden: The Forbidden City*. New York: Scala Publishers, 2008 .

Campbell, Duncan. "Transplanted Peculiarity: the Garden of the Master of the Fishing Nets". *New Zealand Journal of Asian Studies* 9, 1 (2007): 9-25.

Chiu, Che Bing. "Droiture et Clarté: scène paysagère au Jardin de la Clarté Parfaite". *Studies in the History of Gardens & Designed Landscapes*. Chinese Gardens II, 19, 3/4 (1999): 364-375.

Chiu, Che Bing. *Yuan ming yuan: le jardin de la clarté parfaite*. Besançon: Les Éditions de l'Imprimeur, 2000.

Forêt, Philippe. *Mapping Chengde. The Qing Landscape Enterprise*, . Honolulu, Hawai'i: University of Hawai'i Press, 2000.

Hammond, Kenneth J. "Urban Gardens in Ming Jiangnan: Insights from the Essays of Wang Shizhen". In *Gardens, City Life and Culture: A World Tour*, edited by Michel Conan and Chen Wangheng, 41-52. Cambridge, Massachusetts: Harvard University Press, 2008.

Hargett, James M. "Huizong's Magic Marchmount: the Genyue Pleasure Park of Kaifeng". *Monumenta Serica* 38 (1988-1989): 1-48.

Jia, Jun. "Les Jardins du Jiangnan dans l'art paysager à Pékin, pendant les Ming et Qing". In *Le Jardin du lettré: Synthèse des arts en Chine*, edited by Gilles Baud-Berthier, Sophie Couëtoux and Che Bing Chiu, 171-188. Besançon: Les Éditions de l'Imprimeur, 2004.

Li, Gefei. "Famous Gardens of Luoyang". Translation with introduction by Philip Watson. *Studies in the History of Gardens & Designed Landscape*, 24, 1 (2004): 38-54.

Li, June T., ed. *Another World Lies Beyond. Creating Liu Fang Yuan the Huntington's Chinese Garden*. San Marino, California: Huntington Library, 2009.

Liu, Dunzhen. *Chinese Classical Gardens of Suzhou*. Translated by Chen Lixian, edited by Joseph C. Wang. New York: McGraw Hill, 1992.

Markbreiter, Stephen. "Yu Yuan: A Shanghai Garden". *Arts of Asia* 9, 6 (1981): 99-110.

Pirazzoli-t'Serstevens, Michèle, ed. *Le Yuanmingyuan. Jeux d'eau et palais européens du XVIIIe siècle à la cour de Chine*. Paris: Éditions Recherche sur les Civilisations, 1987.

Qian, Yi. *Chinese classical gardens: classical personal gardens in Jiangnan area of China*. Hangzhou: Zhejiang People's Fine Arts Publishing House, 2002.

Wong, Young-Tsu. *A Paradise Lost, the Imperial Garden Yuan ming Yuan*. Honolulu, Hawai'i: University of Hawaii Press, 2001.

Xu, Yinong. "Interplay of Image and Fact: the Pavilion of Surging Waves, Suzhou". *Studies in the History of Gardens & Designed Landscapes*, Chinese Gardens II, 19, 3/4 (1999): 288-301.

Xu, Yinong. "Boundaries, centres and peripheries in Chinese gardens: A case of Suzhou in the eleventh century". *Studies in the History of Gardens & Designed Landscapes* 24, 1 (2004): 21-37.

Xun, Cao. "Le Jardin du Maître du Filet: une histoire au fil de l'eau". In *Le Jardin du lettré: Synthèse des arts en Chine*, edited by Gilles Baud-Berthier, Sophie Couëtoux and Che Bing Chiu, 171-188. Besançon: Les Éditions de l'Imprimeur, 2004.

Yang, Xiaoshan. "Li Deyu's Pingquan Villa: Forming an Emblem from the Tang to the Song". *Asia Maior*, 17, 2 (2004): 45-88.

Yu, Yali (Text) and Rolf Reiner Borchard (Photographs). *Gardens in Suzhou / Gärten in Suzhou*. Stuttgart: Edition Axel Menges, 2003.

Contemporary Landscape Architecture Projects in China

Adam, Hubertus. "Follies am Flussufer". *Archithese* 4 (2007): 40-43.

Belle, Iris. "Beijing Olympic Forest Park. The Axis to Nature". *Topos* 63 (2008): 22-28.

Capezzuto, Rita and Joseph Grima. "Jinhua Architecture Park". *Domus* 894 (2006): 14-29.

Chen, Leslie, and Ryan Lin. "The Hong Kong Wetland Park". *Topos* 55 (2006): 45-49.

Chung, Wah Nan. "La création contemporaine: l'héritage du ting". In *Le Jardin du lettré: Synthèse des arts en Chine*, edited by Gilles Baud-Berthier, Sophie Couëtoux and Che Bing Chiu, 209-217. Besançon: Les Éditions de l'Imprimeur, 2004.

Jaeger, Falk. "Confucius would have loved it". *Topos* 72 (2010): 62-67.

Johnstone, Graham and Kong Xiangfeng. "Making Friends with Floods". *Landscape Architecture* 4 (2007): 106-115.

Laffage, Arnauld. "Public spaces and contemporary gardens". In *In the Chinese city. Perspectives on the transmutations of an empire*, edited by Frédéric Edelmann, 68-75. Barcelona: Actar, 2008.

Liu Hui and Zhao Jing, eds. *Olympic Forest Park Planning and Design*. Beijing: Beijing Tsinghua Urban Planning and Design Institute, 2008.

Padua, Mary G. "Industrial Strength". *Landscape Architecture* 6 (2003): 76-85.

Padua, Mary G. "Style as context: post-traditional open space design in Hong Kong". *Working Paper Series* 164 (2004): 49-70.

Padua, Mary G. "Touching the Good Earth". *Landscape Architecture* 12 (2006): 100-107.

Padua, Mary G. "New traditions and old realities - old traditions and new realities: the emergence of post-Mao park design in China". *Working Paper Series* 190 (2006): 156-180.

Padua, Mary G. "Designing an Identity: the synthesis of a post-traditional landscape vocabulary in Hong Kong". *Landscape Research* 32, 2 (2007): 255-272.

Padua, Mary G. and Kongjian Yu. "China's Cosmetic Cities: urban fever and superficiality". *Landscape Research* 32, 2 (2007): 225-249.

Padua, Mary G. "Contested Chinese Identity: modernism and fundamentalism in contemporary landscape design". *Working Paper Series*. 199 (2008): 1-24.

Padua, Mary G. "A Fine Red Line". *Landscape Architecture* 1 (2008): 91-99.

Selugga, Malte. "The Dragon's Tail". *Topos* 63 (2008): 15-21.

'scape. The international magazine for landscape architecture and urbanism, China's take off, 2 (2010).

"Shanghai Carpet. Shanghai Yang Pu University Hub". In *Groundswell. Constructing the Contemporary Landscape*, edited by Peter Reed, 64-69. Basel: Birkhäuser, 2005.

Stokman, Antje and Stefanie Ruff. "Internationality and Identity". *Topos* 51 (2005): 66-75.

Stokman, Antje and Stefanie Ruff. "Internationality and Identity - the search for a contemporary design idiom in China". In *The art of survival. Recovering landscape architecture*, edited by Kongjian Yu and Mary G. Padua, 53-61. Mulgrave, Victoria: Images Publishing Group, 2006.

Stokman, Antje and Stefanie Ruff. "The Red Ribbon Tanghe River Park. Reconciling Water Management, Landscape Design and Ecology". *Topos* 63 (2008): 29-35.

Valentien, Donata and Christoph. *Shanghai New Botanic Garden / Neuer Botanischer Garten*. Berlin: Jovis, 2008.

Yu, Kongjian and Mary G. Padua, eds. *The art of survival. Recovering landscape architecture*. Mulgrave, Victoria: Images Publishing Group, 2006.

Yu, Kongjian. "Positioning contemporary landscape architecture in China". *Topos* 56 (2006): 91-98.

Yu, Kongjian. "Qiaoyuan Park - An Ecosystem Services-Oriented Regenerative Design". *Topos* 70 (2010): 28-35.

Zhang, Xin, ed. *Suzhou Museum*. Beijing: Great Wall Publishing House, 2008.

AUTHOR'S NOTE
Throughout the book, I have used the Pinyin system for the transliteration of Chinese characters. I have given the name of each garden in Pinyin transliteration followed by an English translation.
I have given Chinese proper names in the traditional order, with the surname first. Where a modern Chinese designer's and/or author's name is known in a different form of transliteration (i.e. Ieoh Ming Pei), I have followed the designer's/author's preferred form.

COLOPHON

GRAPHIC DESIGN & BOOK PRODUCTION
ActarBirkhäuserPro
www.actarbirkhauserpro.com
Barcelona - Basel

BIBLIOGRAPHIC INFORMATION PUBLISHED BY
THE GERMAN NATIONAL LIBRARY
The German National Library lists this publication in the Deutsche Nationalbibliografie; detailed bibliographic data are available on the Internet at http://dnb.d-nb.de.

A CIP catalogue record for this book is available from the Library of Congress, Washington, D.C., USA

This book is also available in a German language edition (ISBN 978-3-0346-0223-5).

© 2011 Birkhäuser GmbH, Basel
P.O. Box, 4002 Basel, Switzerland
Part of ActarBirkhäuser

Printed on acid-free paper produced from chlorine-free pulp. TCF ∞

Printed in Spain

ISBN 978-3-0346-0222-8

9 8 7 6 5 4 3 2 1

www.birkhauser.com

DISTRIBUTION

ActarBirkhäuserD
Barcelona - Basel - New York
www.actarbirkhauser.com
Roca i Batlle 2
E-08023 Barcelona
T +34 93 417 49 93
F +34 93 418 67 07
salesbarcelona@actarbirkhauser.com

Viaduktstrasse 42
CH-4051 Basel
T +41 61 5689 800
F +41 61 5689 899
salesbasel@actarbirkhauser.com

151 Grand Street, 5th floor
New York, NY 10013, USA
T +1 212 966 2207
F +1 212 966 2214
salesnewyork@actarbirkhauser.com